THE USEFULNES

AN AFRICAN PERSPECTIVE

THE USEFULNESS OF DREAMS

An African Perspective

Mary Chinkwita

JANUS PUBLISHING COMPANY
London, England

First published in Great Britain 1993 by
Janus Publishing Company

Copyright © Mary Chinkwita 1993

British Library Cataloguing-in-Publication Data
A catalogue record for this book is
available from the British Library

ISBN 1 85756 046 9

Cover design David Murphy
Phototypeset by Intype, London

Printed & bound in England by
Antony Rowe Ltd, Chippenham, Wiltshire

Dedicated to my mother
LOYA MASEKO CHINKWITA

Contents

Foreword	ix
Acknowledgements	xi
Introduction	xiii
Chapter 1 – Lucid Dreams	1
Chapter 2 – The Author's Dream Experience	30
Chapter 3 – African Societal Beliefs	54
Chapter 4 – Reincarnation Experiences in Dreams	74
Chapter 5 – Dreams in All Ages	90
Chapter 6 – Biblical Dreams	106
Chapter 7 – Dream as a Problem-Solver	119
Conclusion	131
References	132
Index	139

Foreword

It is a great pleasure to introduce to a European public the work of a friend and former student, Miss Mary Chinkwita. She writes on *Dreams* but seeks to show the way in which they are interpreted by many people on the African Continent. Much depends on what you bring to them as an interpreting factor! If you bring the typical scepticism of the average European mind, riddled as it is with rationalism, unbelief, or light humour, then what has been dreamed may not yield anything of great importance, or of personal worth. It will probably get the comment: 'You shouldn't have had so much cheese for supper!'

Or it may be that we hear Martin Luther King's speech, which begins 'I had a dream . . .' and you know that it was not quite a 'dream' in sleep time, but a thought-provoking statement about some revelation of a possible step forward for the underprivileged. We use the word 'dream' too loosely. The word is used quite differently among the native peoples of Australia. The word is used differently in the Bible world. Dreaming there is one of the ways in which God is understood as communicating with men and women. Joseph's life and that of the Children of Israel were saved by the ability of Joseph to interpret dreams as meaningful experiences. So also the dream experience of another Joseph in connection with the Nativity of Jesus, or of Peter and the clean and unclean creatures. Without the 'native' interpretation of those dreams there would have been no Christianity, no movement to include the Gentiles in the story.

Miss Chinkwita has sought to bring to our understanding an awareness of the use of dream from amongst her own people of Malawi, in which insights, interpretations, and people skilled in giving interpretations, play meaningful roles in present-day lives. Having worked with overseas people, particularly from the Third

World, I find it useful to listen to, and to learn from, their interpretations, customs and conventions, before applying European standards. They bring an understanding, and a belief about dreams nearer to the Biblical awareness than to Freud.

I warmly commend this book to all who have dealings with people coming from the Third World and have concerns for their welfare in our society.

Philip B. Cliff (PhD),
Emeritus Head of the Church Education Section,
Westhill College,
Birmingham

Acknowledgements

A special vote of thanks is due to Dr Charles Kafumba for his forbearance in editing the original draft manuscript. His comments and insight proved highly invaluable in organising and reflecting on my initial thoughts and ideas. I would also like to thank Revd Dr Philip Cliff, Brian Ragbourn and Miss Pat Bryden for their precious suggestions and just that extra ready helping hand. Thanks are also due to Angela Kafumba and Grace and John Jal-Wang for their encouragement.

Thanks to my colleague at Parkside Hostel, both the residents and the staff, for their contribution and encouragement – Barbara Lee, and Margaret Kewley, to mention but a few. I would also like to thank my friends at Liverpool Social Services for their contribution, support and encouragement: Sue McGuire, Peter Dowd, Angela Glanville, May Mills, Phil Purvis, Dorothy Wescombe and Mike Huett. Their ideas and suggestions were very much appreciated. Everyone contributed and one person had to put those ideas on the paper. My thanks to Patti Dewhirst for helping with the typing of the first draft.

In addition I would like to thank my colleagues at Earle Road (URC) for their support: Revd Wilson Morris, Mrs Dorothy Fellows and Miss Sybil Holmes, to mention but a few. Thanks also to Revd Ken Pattison and Sue, his wife (Presbyterian Church, Edinburgh), for their help; also to Evelyn Jones for reading the first draft.

A number of people both in Malawi and the United Kingdom have contributed in many different ways towards the compilation of this book. Thanks in particular to Sandra St Rose and the dreamers whose names appear. It would, however, be a great oversight if I did not mention my mother, to whom this book is dedicated. She gave me some dreams to add to my book; and my brother, Stensfield Chinkwita, for his sustained encouragement.

Introduction

This book focuses on the usefulness of natural lucid dreams.*
These kinds of dreams are contrasted with those obtained under
controlled laboratory environments, or sleeping laboratories, as
they are commonly known in dream literature. Their usefulness
is seen in prophecy and personal, as well as cultural, problem-
solving. The book also offers a very effective way of recording
dreams.

With the use of African and some English case studies, I shall
show that dreams are a natural process in an individual's life and
that they affect the lives of the dreamers and/or those who have
been dreamt about.

I am of the contention that dreams taken in sleeping laboratories
are somehow induced and are therefore artificial. The subjects are
put under hypnosis in the laboratory. Their dreams are recorded
and the subjects are woken up at intervals and asked what they
had been dreaming about. It could be argued that this artificial
environment can result in 'disturbing' dreams which, in turn,
could cause undue distress to the subject, while in natural lucid
dreams the actors have traditionally woken up of their own accord
and have had time to recall their dream experiences in a leisurely
way. In natural lucid dreams no one wakes you up. It happens
automatically. This is probably because the actors are not influenced by the often frightening laboratory devices. Nor are they
subjected to disturbing alarm-bells which inhibit the flow of their
dreams. Thus, since dreams are sweetest in the morning hours,
the laboratory dreamer fails to appreciate the dignity of dreams
and their interpretive power.

I therefore refute the concept of hypnotism, since dreams ought

---

* Natural dreams which come at a particular time when the gods want to send a
  message to human beings. (Lucid = being aware that one is dreaming.)

to be natural and are sent from the gods. Thus, every kind of dream, be it seemingly trivial, nonsensical or illogical when analysed, brings a message of its own. Natural dreams originate from the subconscious mind. The subconscious in this case becomes the realm or stage on which dreams are performed. The lingering memory of the dream remains in the conscious mind and when the dreamer awakes the dream can be contemplated or analysed. Thus Keith Hearne (*New Scientist*, 24 September 1981) page 783 argues that, 'objects and people appear to be, and feel, solid and the lucid dreamer is able to converse intelligently with the dream characters.'

Although lucid dreams fit in with both the internalist and externalist theories of dreams, the case studies presented in this book seem to strongly support the externalist view. Thus, as will become clear later, the Temiar (people from Malaysia, also known as the Senoi) are able in their dreams to manipulate events and direct their dream content. I will also look at the history of Rapid Eye Movement (REM) research.

This book was written as a result of my childhood dream premonitions of my father dying, and of myself and my father being beaten to the point of death. That these two events actually predicted the future commended my respect for dreams and their contents. I find dreams very useful and meaningful and I have frequently been guided by dreams. In order to provide a clear framework of understanding of the wide-ranging issues affecting the dream work and how it affects us, the present work has been divided into seven chapters.

I begin with a review of existing literature in the first chapter, where lucid dreams are analysed and situated within the following conceptual frameworks:

(a) Freud's 'wish-fulfilment' theory, which looks at dreams as an expression of what would otherwise be inexpressible through various day-to-day constraints of the society within which the actors live.

(b) The externalist approach, which views dreams as emanating from external forces which work on the dreamer. Jung's work falls persistently within this school of thought.

(c) The internalist school of thought, which argues that dreams originate from within the self – Adler *et al*.

Operationally important proponents of this theoretical approach, including definitions of lucid dreams and natural lucid dreams, are offered and distinction between them drawn. These are contrasted with sleep-laboratory-induced dreams.

The second half of Chapter 1 looks at the concept of lucid dreams, with illustrations taken from among the Temiar of Malaysia. These are compared with those of the people of Malawi, in southern Africa.

Chapter 2 describes in detail the writer's own experiences, both in Africa as a child and in Britain, where these dreams were recorded. It is here that we see the central reality of dreams in day-to-day life and in important decision-making.

My dream experiences are compared with those of a Sudanese lady who accurately predicted in her dreams the future of my friend Grace Jal-wang.

Chapter 3 looks at the wider context of African societal beliefs. It is traditionally believed in Africa that dreams occur at a particular time when the gods want to reveal something which is unknown to human beings. Thus, dreams always have a purpose. They convey future messages or warning of impending dangers. Ancestors act as intermediaries. People in Africa have been cured of sickness by listening to dreams and dream messages.

Chapter 4 looks at Barbara Lee's dreams concerning reincarnation. Dreams helped her to believe she had existed before. This chapter examines other case studies as well, although not necessarily on reincarnation.

Chapter 5 looks at examples of compelling dreams associated with such prominent philosophers as Plato, Hippocrates *et al*. The argument here is that the dream, whether we like it or not, will continue to exist in every society. Dreams have conditioned human perceptions, and as such have influenced people of all ages.

Chapter 6 examines biblical dreams taken from both the Old Testament and the New. Dreams from other world religions are also examined.

Chapter 7 looks at the dream as a problem-solver. The interpretation of dreams as problem-solving is a theory which started fifty years ago in the West; but it presumably started much earlier among the aborigines of Australia, Africa and India. Some of the dreams here are also the writer's own dream experiences on problem-solving; some are on the subject of telepathy.

Chapter 1

Lucid Dreams

At first sight the dream world seems to be completely removed from a person's day-to-day activities and emotional feelings. An historical review of the role of dreams, however, reveals that dreams can be just as important as any of the familiar five biological senses that endow man with eyesight, hearing, tasting, smelling and feeling. Dreams offer the potential for an extra sixth sense which, in unison and compatibility with the other senses, can guide, forewarn and predict events in a man's life.

Dream content and its interpretation differ in space and time. This attribute is fully reflected in the different perceptions and functional definitions offered by various authors. Sutherland, in his review 'Mixing Memory and Desire', summarises definitions given by these authors. For instance, Freud has argued that the function of dreams is simply to reveal our true selves and unconscious desires. Jung argues that there are a number of archetypes in the collective unconscious that the majority of people have access to. Authors like Francis Crick posit a more divine definition, arguing that dreams are messages from the gods. Peter Medawar proposes that they are the result of the mind free-wheeling; that they are a method of solving problems; and that their contents are irrelevant.[1]

It is not my intention in the present book to make value judgments about who is right or wrong. Rather, my task is to examine a particular type of dream, called 'lucid', and illustrate through case studies how these have actually guided and helped humanity.

This chapter looks at the concept of lucid natural dreams, with illustrations taken from among the Temiar people of Malaysia. The Temiars' way of looking at dreams is compared to that of the Malawians. It must, however, be pointed out that the majority of some African countries is an amalgamation of cross-cultural politics whose characteristics, in terms of cultural orientations, are variable; using countries or states as sociological analytical frameworks tends to obscure a number of important social phenomena central to a study of this type. On the other hand we need also to point out that the cultural gaps which existed in these original groupings have since narrowed down due to intercultural marriages and the mass-cultural socialisation process which is an integral part of modern states. Even with this new understanding it would be too large an analytical block to examine dreams and dreams interpretation within the context of a national perspective. I have therefore restricted my area of study to the Ngoni of central Malawi.

The term 'lucid dreaming', as Susan Blackmore puts it (*New Scientist*, 6 January 1990), was first used by Frederick Van Eeden, a Dutch psychiatrist, in 1913. He stated that, in this sort of dream, the reintegration of the psychic functions is so complete that the sleeper reaches a stage of perfect awareness and is able to direct her/his attention, and to attempt different acts of free volition. Yet the sleep, as I am able confidently to state, is undisturbed, deep and refreshing.[2] Lucid dreams, therefore, are those in which the dreamer is fully aware of the fact that he/she is dreaming. Hearne defines lucid dreams as those of a remarkable type, in which the subject becomes perfectly aware, while asleep, that he/she is dreaming, and can then, to a large extent, control the content of the dream and its course of action.[3] He further observes that the character of lucid dreams is like being awake, having 'free will' and possessing 'critical faculties', but being in a totally artificial 'other' world – and knowing so.[4] To clarify the meaning of lucid dreams, Susan Blackmore, in the *Sunday Times* of 3 June 1990, page 17, reports the finding of LaBerge and his team at Stanford University that 'a lucid dream (although its centuries-old name implies otherwise) need not always be vivid, rather it is a dream in which you know, at the time, that it is a dream.'[5] Thus, as we have seen, true lucidity simply means knowing that one is actually dreaming. To understand the true meaning of lucid dreaming it is helpful to examine specific dream experiences.

Peter Dowd, aged thirty-three, a Development Officer of the Liverpool Social Services, gives the following personal experience of his own lucid dream.

'I have always been interested in dreams. I am not sure that they have any significance. However, they can be used, I believe, for purposes of recreation. I use them in two ways. Firstly, I try to control my dream by "flying". I am able to fly about house high and sometimes higher. I can achieve this regularly and fairly easily. I eventually try to go higher for longer periods or else I become more versatile. Secondly, I enjoy reading Conan Doyle and I have tried to accompany Holmes and Watson on detective cases! I have so far managed to follow part of a case, but have only been able to "watch" and not participate fully as I would like. I intend to try and participate once again as I become more adept at it.'

According to my experience, the lucid dream takes a second characteristic of vividity. Colours are normally brighter than usual. This aspect of lucid dreams will be explored in subsequent chapters.

Orthodox scientists who study sleep, according to Susan Blackmore, argue that lucid dreams could not possibly be real dreams at all. The very idea of awareness in a dream is viewed as a contradiction. They state that lucid dreams must be occurring in brief moments of wakefulness or in the transition between waking and sleeping but not in the kind of deep sleep during which rapid eye movement (REMs) and ordinary dreams usually take place.[6]

It has proved to be a problem for lucid dreamers to convince orthodox scientists, because there seems to be a convergence of opinion that the human body is to some extent paralysed during sleep. Hearne, who has done much research on sleep, realised that 'not all your muscles are paralysed. In REM sleep, the eyes move. So perhaps a lucid dreamer could signal with eye movements'.[7] Blackmore also reports that researchers both in Britain and America emphasise on the same issue that 'the muscles, though paralysed, twitch with dream actions. It is as though the brain is actively planning thoughts and movements while the paralysis stops them from being acted out – perhaps allowing you to do things which would be too threatening in real life.'[8] Alan Worsley, a lucid dreamer, is quoted by Blackmore as having managed to play a crucial trick. 'He decided to move his eyes left and right eight times in succession whenever he realised he was dreaming.' In the sleep laboratory, Hearne had him connected to a polygraph and could see the string of extreme eye movements clearly recorded in the middle of REM sleep.'[9] This showed that the doubters were wrong. Lucid dreams are real dreams and do occur during REM sleep.

Although some people indeed doubt the existence of lucid dreams, the present author does not. In 1989 I administered a questionnaire to members of staff at Parkside, in Liverpool, a hostel for the physically handicapped. Out of twenty people interviewed, eighteen said they always knew when they were dreaming. One of the remaining two, Maggie McDermott, said she did not know when she dreamt. The other one, Gladys Marriott, said she did not remember a single dream and that she did not even know whether she dreamt at all.

In a survey of university students, Green (1966), as quoted by Keith Hearne, found that seventy-three per cent of the sample answered 'yes' to the simple question: 'Have you ever had a dream in which you were aware that you were dreaming?' (70/95 males, 14/15 females).[10]

In most cases lucid natural dreams are useful and meaningful and they normally convey a message. When analysing the dream content one sees the message it is portraying, no matter how complicated. Peter Dowd gives another account of a dream which he thought at first was meaningless, but in the end discovered was dreamt for a reason. This is the dream in Peter's own words:

While on holiday in Scotland some eleven years ago, I experienced an unusual dream. I was staying at a small hotel with a friend. We were on a coach holiday. On Wednesday night, following our arrival at the hotel, I went to bed after having a couple of drinks. I did not drink heavily, though. During the early hours of Thursday morning, I woke feeling rather hot and a little disturbed. I could not quite describe what I had dreamt, other than that I saw in my room, or in my sleep, a green presence. It was no more than that. The green appeared to drift across my area of vision. My friend was awakened because of my disturbance. I said little and went back to sleep.

The following morning I explained to him what I had experienced. I thought more about it but I vividly remembered the overwhelming sense of 'green'. I related the story to no one else. Some days later, on our way home, the coach-driver told us a story about the hotel we had been to.

It happened that the hotel had, some two hundred years earlier, been the house of an old laird. A serving-girl took the laird's eye and she became his unwilling mistress. The woman continued to see her young lover from another village regularly. The old laird found out and one night followed her into the garden. He shot her and as she died she told the old laird that she had visited her young lover to tell him that she was ending their affair because the old laird had been good to her and she had fallen in love with him. However, before she expired she also told the laird that she would haunt the house as long as a Campbell lived in it. She died in the laird's arms just on the spot in the garden where an annexe to the hotel had been built. My bedroom was in the annexe where she died. One final twist in the tale: the young woman has often haunted the laird's house and had become known as 'the woman in green' on account of the colour of the dress she often wore and which she was wearing on the night of her death.

In this case, Peter did not know anything about the past history of this hotel. He had no prior knowledge.

As we can see, although Peter initially found the dream rather trivial, he later came to learn, after the driver's story, its true significance. The dream was revealing to Peter the past history of the place he had slept in. Dreams are therefore dreamt for a reason. They reveal hidden incidents. Thus, the elements that go to make a dream are different from most of our waking thoughts.

Dream laboratory

People can experience lucid dreams either in sleeping laboratories or in the privacy of their bedrooms. The only distinction is that those in the laboratory are to some extent induced. I find this rather unethical since they can cause all sorts of physiological, as well as psychological, problems. The inducement factor also means that the dreams are incomplete, as the messages may not be reliably forthcoming, since the subject is put under hypnosis in the laboratory. First he is made familiar with the environment. He is then connected by three electrical recording tracings. These monitor the subject when asleep. The electoencephalogram (EEG) records the 'brainwaves'. The electrooculogram (EOG) records the movement of the eyes and the electromyogram (EMG) reflects general body muscles tone.

After the instrumentation of the subject is complete, the researcher knows the subject is dreaming through observing the rapid eye movement (REMs). It is through the eye movement that the subject communicates with the researcher.

Perhaps the most profound is given by Raymond de Becker (1968) in his book *The Understanding of Dreams*. De Becker's experiments took place in a Moscow laboratory. The patient was put to sleep under hypnosis and given a topic, e.g. a walk in the desert. He was also informed that he was sleeping and that he was dreaming. An EEG recorded the oscillations of the brain. The standard stimulus was that of 'a test-tube of oil of turpentine near the patient, touching his cheek with a test-tube full of ice, doing the same with a test-tube full of water at sixty degrees, and the same again with fine wire wool, whistling on specific frequences, switching on an electric torch with the beam directed upon the face, arm or clenched fingers of the patient'.[11]

After waking up, the patient did not normally remember that he had been put to sleep by hypnosis; he didn't even remember that the theme had been suggested to him. There are also circumstances where a patient is not given a guide. A female patient who was not given any guidance, but her cheek was touched for three seconds with a test-tube full of warm water, reported to have dreamt of her childhood.[12]

Another patient who had the same stimulus dreamt of being arrested by police. This was because he had broken the traffic rules. The policeman wanted him to pay on the spot.

A further interesting dream from de Becker is that of the 'ultra-paradoxical phase'. 'The patient, after being touched on the cheek with a test-tube of warm water, dreamt that he was walking in an icy forest in winter. In the distance was a fire, which he could not reach. That is clearly the inversion of sensations as described in the Pavlovian theory of the 'ultra-paradoxical' functioning of the nervous system.'[14]

In some cases a patient under the influence of hypnosis related his dream when asked. He did this without being awakened. He was asked again to relate his dream experience when he was awake and it was not disclosed to him that he had already been asked. 'The two accounts tallied absolutely, which would indicate that the patient did not have time to invent them,' as de Becker puts it. It is true he did not invent them, but one could argue that the subject in most cases dreamt of the things he had already seen before being put to sleep.

To explain further about what happens in the laboratory, I will give Jerry's examples. Jerry and Don were put in the laboratory, as stated by R. D. Cartwright in *Night Life* (1977). Their dreams were recorded on the same night. They were both in their twenties and were both intelligent medical students. They could remember that they had usually dreamt only once a week in their private dreams.

First they slept in the laboratory for two nights without being awakened, so that they became familiar with the EEG monitoring. They were then told the experiments would keep on awakening them on the night of actual recording and that they should report any mental activity happening to them. The awakenings were made at intervals. The first was five minutes after the onset of the first REM sign; the rest of the awakenings were made after ten minutes. In the morning the subjects were asked to review a few dreams. I will deal with Jerry's dreams only, since this is merely a matter of showing an example of what goes on in the laboratory.

Dream 1

Upon awakening for the first time, he reported: 'I was playing with the leads from these electrodes in my mind, and trying to figure out where they went. I was pulling out plugs and putting others back in there. There didn't seem to be any real order to it. I can't really remember a whole lot. I know I played around for a while. I stuck the leads in once and they didn't seem to be right, so I put them in a different way. I do remember seeing a picture and I had them all stuck in a little box down at this end. (*Question – You saw a picture?*) Well, in a mental image, what the terminal box looked like which I stuck the leads into.'[16]

Dream 2

In the second dream, Jerry was with his friends driving a car. He could remember the streets and the stop signs. There was no snow on the ground and not many buildings. Don, his friend, was also there and Mr H. They had Mr H.'s Volkswagen. Later Jerry said Mr H. was not there. He remembered they were going to the laboratory.

The reality of this dream is that Jerry had been driven to the laboratory along with the other students, including Don, by a laboratory assistant, and Mr H., who was driving a van. Mr H. was actually there, but Jerry thought he was not.

Dream 3

When he was awakened for the third time, Jerry remembered that he was going to the Chicago public library. The library looked like the University of Illinois at Champaign. The library looked like the one he had known during his undergraduate days. There was also a bit of the future element in this dream. The library was in the location of the hospital where Jerry might have some opportunity in future of doing his 'practicals' while undertaking his medical studies.

Dream 4

He dreamt he was making mud pies; a girl whom he couldn't remember was helping him. It was a bright, sunny day. The pies looked pretty and he was using a paint-stirring stick as a brush. The mud was brown. It was a kind of brown mud.

This was like remembering his childhood playing with the mud. This is also like a wish-fulfilment dream, as propounded by Freud: playing with sand and making mud pies with the help of a little girl.

Dream 5

His mum was giving him a bath. He remembered having seen a sink and his mum had water in it which she used for washing his face, and she had a hold of his earlobe and was pulling it and cleaning inside his ears.

This dream looks like wish-fulfilment too, because in dreams 1, 2 and 3 Jerry expressed it as hard to take care of everything in a new and sophisticated world. In dream 4 he wished he was small, and in this last dream it looked as if he was concluding that it was better to be small so that his mother could take care of him. 'The emotional tone is wrong, though', as Cartwright puts it. He is not enjoying being cared for. The symbolic mum is his experimenter; the experimenter reports that he scrubbed his earlobes with a white sponge soaked in acetone which he told Jerry was for cleaning his skin.

Most of Jerry's dreams were concerned with the past and the present. But if I was to examine Don's dreams we would have seen one of the dreams referring to the future. He dreamt of withdrawing money for a holiday in France. Cartwright asserts that 'the nature of a night's dream activity cannot be called random'. Dreams begin with feelings and the concern the person was experiencing just before sleep. The problem with laboratory dreams is that the subject is interrupted in the middle of the dream. This makes it difficult to see the dream's final end.

Those taking place in private are those which I have called 'natural lucid dreams', in the sense that the dreamer has not been 'prepared' to dream. With the laboratory ones there is much preparation. The subjects are in the laboratory familiarising themselves with the new environment, while in the natural ones people sleep in the privacy of their own homes, peacefully and comfortably in their beds. A dream comes unexpectedly. Normally they come at specific times and bring messages of their own. Messages vary – time and space. Depending on the individual's circumstances, dreams may come to encourage us in times of anxiety and depression. They guide us when we go astray and warn us of the future. Central to natural dreams is the element of impromptu or spontaneous generation and that they come to tell us something of which we are not aware, as we shall see in Chapter 2.

Natural dreams, however, come of their own accord. Green (1963), as quoted by Hearne, was prepared to include under the term 'lucid dreams' visual/imaginal phenomena of the waking state. And if the subject experienced vivid imagery, these dreams could be examples of unusual hypnagogic and hyponomic imagery.[17]

The question raised by the orthodox scientists earlier on is debatable. Malcolm in his book *Dreaming* (1959), considered states resembling sleep and concluded that hypnosis, for instance, is not sleep. Also, commenting on the link between REM sleep and the great number of dream reports on waking from that stage to others, he points out that stage REM should not be used as a criterion.[18]

While these arguments are valid, M. Jouvet in his article 'The States of Sleep' (*Scientific American*, 1967) asserts that 'now it has been known for nearly two decades that the brain contains a centre specifically responsible for maintaining wakefulness'.[19] This was discovered by H. W. Magoun of the US, and Giuseppe Moruzzi of Italy, working together at North-Western University in 1957. They named this centre, located in mid-brain, the 'Reticular Activisting System' (RAS). Cats were used in their experiments.[20] To comment on this part of the brain which does not sleep, an elderly man, Stan Ruddock, told me, while I was conducting my research in Britain, that there is a part of our mind which is not used during the conscious hours. It is only active, or operates, during sleep.

However, the findings of Magoun *et al.* could be said to show that the part of the brain which does not sleep during the night is responsible for the function of the dream. This could only work if people reasoned like Adler, that a dream is just what someone had been thinking during the previous day, and also that dreams come from within, as we shall see later. The problem is, dreams tell us about the future and things of which we are not aware, but if this is the case then it could be said that the part which remains awake does not really deal with the dream function.

Nathaniel Kleitman in his article 'Patterns of Dreaming' (1960), denotes that dreams are accompanied by certain characteristics, types of brainwave and REM. This was discovered by a graduate named Eugene Aserinsky, who observed an infant sleeping and found major body movement ceased with the onset of sleep, except for the eyes. The eye movements would stop and begin again from time to time and were the first movements to be seen when the infant woke up.[21]

He suggested eye movements can be used in adults as well, following similar cycles. Disturbance to sleepers was minimised by monitoring the eye movement remotely with an EEG, a device that records the weak electrical signals generated continuously by the brain. The difference across the eyeball between the cornea and the retina makes it possible to detect movements of the eyes by means of electrodes taped to the skin above and below on either side of the eye. These tracings of the EEG showed not only the slow movements of the eyes that Aserinsky had observed in infants but also REMs that came in clusters. Each individual eye movement took a fraction of a second, but a cluster often lasted, with interruptions, as long as fifty minutes.[22]

Scientists currently believe that seemingly lengthy dreams occur in a flash. For example, Alfred Maury, in the last century, dreamt a long and complicated dream leading to his being beheaded at the guillotine. On waking, terrified, he found that the bedhead had fallen on his neck and concluded that the whole dream had been created in that moment.[23]

There seems to be a general consensus, though. Nerys Dee (1984) states that during the night we progress through a series of sessions of approximately ninety minutes. Throughout these the NREM (see below) and REM states alternate. They commence at stage 1 with NREM sleep and then move into further NREM stages 2, 3, 4 and 5. These are followed by a phase of REM dreaming. This pattern repeats itself during the night, depending on how much sleep is needed. Towards the morning NREM sleep decreases and REM sleep increases.[24]

Nathaniel Kleitman also states that in some cases the subjects reported they had been dreaming during periods when they showed no rapid eye movements. Others moved their bodies restlessly when the records on the other channels of EEG indicated they were dreaming. Sometimes the heart and respiration claimed to have been dreaming when his dream waves indicated a deeper phase of sleep.[25]

Another technique as Susan Blackmore puts it, is the one that needs all the gadgets. The basic principles is to use some kind of external signal to remind people, during REM sleep, that they are dreaming. Blackmore adds that Hearne first tried spraying water on sleepers' hands and faces but eventually settled for a mild electric shock to the wrist. His 'dream machine' detected periods of REM by monitoring changes in breathing rate, delivering the shocks automatically.[26]

Stephen LaBerge, as Susan Blackmore puts it, rejected taped voices and vibrations and finally designed the 'dreamlight', a machine that detects the eye movement of REM sleep and turns on flashing lights when they reach a certain level. To test the effectiveness of LaBerge's machine, forty-four people came into his laboratory, most of them for just one night, and more than half of them had at least one lucid dream. Two people had their first lucid dream in this way. This, as Blackmore puts it, seems to be the most successful. The availability of induction techniques means there are even more subjects who can take part in experiments to learn more about lucid dreams.[27]

However, Nerys Dee (1984) asserts that with the refinement of electronics came more and more detailed recordings of the brain's activity. By the 1950s two distinct sleep states, dreaming and non-dreaming, had created a lot of contradictions in determining what is non-REM and what is REM. As a consequence every researcher had his own pet name for dreaming and non-dreaming sleep. It was later discovered that rapid sleep are referred to as non-REM (NREM), and REM sleep states. According to Nerys Dee, 'These and other recordable physiological impulses and patterns are now collectively known as biofeedback data.'[28]

Conceptual framework of lucid dreams

A. Sigmund Freud, 1856–1939

Freud's theory of dreaming centred on human behaviour and a distinction between the conscious and unconscious. He named the unconscious 'Id' and argues that this seeks to gratify basic instincts, especially sex and aggression. The conscious mind – the 'ego', as he called it – regulates interaction with the surrounding environment. He came up with a third element in human instinct, which he called the 'superego'. Freud's superego represents the moral demands of the community. During sleep the 'ego' is absent so the 'Id' then brings vicarious gratification through dreams. Freud considered dreams to be the 'Royal Road' to the knowledge of the unconscious in mental life. Thus he believed dreams are the means by which the individual can give room to fantasies and fears which would be totally unacceptable in waking life.[29] Freud seems to have been greatly influenced by the work of the ancient Greek philosopher, Plato, who regarded dreams as the place where the bestial side of man could safely vent its anger without fear of damage.[30]

Freud adds that dream symbols exist in order to disguise the real meaning of the dream, lest the message alarm the sleeper and awaken him prematurely.[31] The main thrust of Freud's theory of dreams are that they fulfil our wishes and that they come from within ourselves. He believed that whatever messages a dream brings, be it death, violence or love, it is all wishfulfilment. Freud was so personally attached to this theory that he allowed subjectivity to influence his dream interpretation. He was so dogmatic that he could not let anyone disagree with his particular interpretation. For example, when in 1895 a patient produced a dream that seemingly contradicted his theory, Freud responded by saying, 'Thus it was her wish that I might be wrong, and her dream showed that wish-fulfilment'.[32]

Freud's interpretation of dreams as 'wish-fulfilling', however, needs to be put into context. Ann Faraday (1972) asserts that Freud had a dream himself. In his dream he was sitting on the terrace of the Bellevue Hotel in Vienna pondering a dream of the previous night in which an hysterical patient of his, Irma, told him she still had pains and was far from cured. She looked so ill in the dream that Freud became alarmed and thought he must have overlooked some organic sickness. His colleagues reached the same conclusion and said she was suffering from an infection as a result of an injection administered by Freud's colleague, 'Otto', with a dirty syringe.

The dream had obviously been sparked off by the fact that on the evening before, Otto had actually visited Freud and told him that he had seen Irma on holiday and that she looked better but not well.[33] Freud thought he detected a note of reproach in Otto's voice and carried over his anxieties into sleep.

Freud spent much time analysing this dream. But the major revelation, which hit him in a blinding flash of insight as he sat on the terrace, and which has since become the foundation of psychoanalytical practice and theory, was of the motive for the wish.[34] 'The dream', Freud wrote, 'fulfilled certain wishes which were started in me by the events of the previous evening.'[35] Freud concluded that he was not responsible for the persistence of Irma's pains, but that Otto was.

Freud-type dreams are indeed common even today. For instance, a girl called Jackie Langley, aged sixteen, told me of a startling dream experience. She used to dream of a boy whom she fancied. All her dreams were dominated by dreams of this boy.

Another girl, who wanted to remain anonymous, told me that she used to have a dream of a boy she wanted to marry. The girl works in a youth hostel in Liverpool as an Assistant Officer. During the night she had the most vivid dream she had ever had. In the dream someone rang the bell of her door. She went to open the door only to find it was this boy in a white suit. She kissed the boy and asked him to come in. The girl went to make a cup of tea and gave it to him. Later the boy vanished. To her disappointment she got up to find that she was at her place of work. She thought she was in her flat. The persistence of this dream was so strong that it could even occur to her while awake (day-dreaming).

It is also very common for schoolchildren to dream about flying, particularly after they have examinations. Flying is normally associated with success and in this particular case passing examinations.

Consequently, in some respects Freud's theory cannot be totally ignored. It should, however, be noted that it is not all-encompassing. That is, it does not accommodate the whole range of dream circumstances, as will become clear in this book.

For instance, Freud was faced with the problem of explaining fear and anxiety dreams as wish-fulfilments.[36] As K. M. T. Hearne puts it, he pleaded that the dream work may have been incompetent so that direct latent material is presented, or that the fulfilment of the wish itself provokes anxiety, or that the censor has been overpowered by strong 'Id' forces.

However, he strongly linked the process of dreaming to that of the unconscious mind at work and play. He was the first to establish that sleep is not a coma-like condition but the active process of a mind awake. He also emphasised that dreams relate to events both immediate and from the buried past of the dreamer.[37]

However, Freud met with opposition. Some authors claimed that his theory was unscientific. Hearne quoted Popper, who once argued that the psychoanalytic theory, including dream theory was a myth and that it was easily verifiable but not readily falsifiable.[38]

B. Carl Gustav Jung, 1875–1961

Jung was Freud's student. Their relationship was so strong that Jung looked to Freud as his father. Freud actually wrote to Jung in April 1909 to say that he formally adopted him as his eldest son.[39] They worked together for some time but eventually Jung found it hard to continue working with Freud and started out on his own.

In his work, Jung established himself as a major critic of Freud. For instance, he disagreed with Freud's belief that sexual repression was the underlying stimulating cause of dreams. Jung argued that the sexual theory was an unproven hypothesis whose applicability and adequacy were only temporal and could not possibly be preserved as an article of faith for all time. Jung initially supported Freud especially on the theory of unconsciousness, but later decided to go his own way. He did not agree with Freud on the theory of the dream being derived from the sexual instinct, as indicated above.

Freud and Jung disagreed on a number of other points. First, while Freud saw dreams as a device to distort or disguise the true dream message, Jung saw dreams as an integral part of human behaviour which did not intend to deceive but rather to express something.[40] According to Jung, dream gives a true picture of individualisation, by which he meant that working with our dreams helps us to reintegrate the whole of our personalities and so become more complete persons.

Secondly, Jung saw the unconscious as being different from the conscious of our dreams. He also saw the symbols of our dreams as carrying messages from the instinctive part of our nature to the rational mind. Indeed, he took the symbols as facts from which we must proceed.

Thirdly, he did not agree with Freud's contention that dream goes back to infantile sexual wishes or to 'the land of childhood'. Freud described this period as when the consciousness was not yet separated from the 'collective unconscious'. But Jung rather saw dreams as foretelling the future. For Jung, dreams make us more whole by using images that tell us about part of ourselves that we ignore, suppress or simply do not want to know. And so our unconscious is a partner, not an opposing force. He saw dreams as a natural being; a vast reservoir of the unknown. In other words, he saw dreams as coming from outside our mind, and believed that their contents are significant.

This is supported by the dream experiences of Pat Bryden, a college lecturer in her forties, who at thirteen dreamt that her mother was going to have a baby. She confessed she did not know at the particular time how a pregnant woman looked or how babies were made. She thinks her mother was probably already pregnant when she had this dream. By then her mother had only two children, a brother and herself. She was the younger of the two. It seemed improbable that the family could have expected any other children.

In the very same dream she discovered that her parents had sold their house and gone to live in the countryside. Years later her dream was realised. Her mother had a baby boy and Pat was fond of pushing the pram. Her parents also sold their house and went to live in the country. Her dream remains a puzzle to her to this day and she wonders why she had this kind of dream. It follows, then, that dreams can predict the future. Dreams said Jung, tell us exactly 'how the matter stands', and nothing else.

Fourthly, Jung saw dreams as one of balancing or compensation to maintain or restore harmony to the whole being. He took dreams as something beyond the realm of the personal unconscious to tap into what he referred to as the collective unconscious. He felt that at the deepest layers of our unconsciousness there are certain symbols which are familiar to the whole human race. These are genetically embodied in us, and they give a response during critical moments in life.

These responses then appear in consciousness, in the form of what he called 'archetypal imagery'. The archetype itself is the inherited predisposition. The imagery derived from them has much in common with myths, folklore and superstitions, e.g. images of creation, paradise, the earth mother, the powerful father and the monster. Jung regarded these as of great importance and indicative of major shifts in the dreamer's unconscious.

These images, or archetypes, exist in our unconscious mind. One of my workmates, Mary Durgan, aged fifty-two was standing by the stairs in her house when she encountered her mother, who had died many years before. Her mother beckoned to her. She thought she really had seen her mother. Later she realised it was only hypnogogic. This dream just came out of nowhere. Archetypes appear in day-dreams. One explanation for archetypes in dreams is that primordial images form part of an inherited ancestral memory,[41] as we have seen in Mary's case.

Fifthly, Jung felt we should see dreams as natural events bearing messages that are meant to be understood.[42] I am inclined to agree with Jung. Dreams ought to be taken as natural and come at particular times when 'the gods' want to send a message. Dreams are natural, they are part of our lives. They give us a sense of direction. They need not be induced. They bring a message which is unknown to us.

Although Jung's theory sounds convincing, he met with criticisms, especially of his notion of dream as a compensatory message. It is said to be rather like the Roman belief that dreams were messages from the gods, which was challenged by Cicero, the rebellious, who asked, 'Why, if the gods can warn us of impending events in dreams, should they not do so when we are awake?'[43] This is debatable. It is only during sleep, when everything is quiet, that the message can be bestowed upon us, as we shall see in Chapter 3. However, many shamas claim to experience trance states in which they can communicate with the spirits: not necessarily in a dream state but during the day as well.

Alfred Adler 1870–1937

Adler was under the impression that waking thoughts are similar to sleeping ones. For this reason he believed that dreams are a continuation of our waking life. As R. D. Cartwright et al put it, 'Dreams are not in opposition to the thoughts of waking life, but a continuation of it'.[44] For Adler, 'Dreams have a "future orientation" arising out of unfinished business: they deal with problems not yet solved.'[45] But, like those who believe that our body is paralysed during sleep, Adler was prepared to say that, whether sleeping or waking, thoughts are similar; the thoughts in sleep, however, are indications of deficiency.

He did not accept the concept of the unconscious in the way Freud and Jung did. Nor did he accept Freud's sexuality theory in dreams. He concentrated on the theory of superiority complexes.

These beliefs originated from observing what he called 'Organ Inferiority'.[46] This he called a physical defect or deformation, leading to over-compensation of the personality.

To illustrate this, he gave an example of small men who were always dominant in society thanks to their effort to comply with a driving compensation complex. But if a goal was too far removed from reality and they failed in their attempt to reach it, they became victims of a nervous breakdown, making excuses like: If only I did not have that I would have succeeded.[47] Adler stated that this kind of thing is not manifested in dreams. Like Freud, Adler believed dreams occur when people are troubled by some unresolved problems during waking life. Many therapists also believe that dreams deal with our most important personal emotional concerns, concerns that we may still know little about.

The Senoi

The Senoi are people found in the Malay Peninsula and in small groups along the coastal plains of Siak, in Sumatra, Indonesia. The Senoi language, also called Sakai, is a member of the group of the Austro-Asiatic language family which includes Semai in the centre, Jah Hut in the East and Temiar in the North.[48] They live in communal houses and have some degree of political development. They are active in hunting, fishing and food-gathering.

I have chosen the Senoi people because, according to Noone (1962), as quoted by Holman, 'the entire lives of [the Senoi] are dominated by their dreams'.[49] Moreover, the Senoi themselves claim that there has hardly been a violent crime. They have over a long period not had any cross-border conflicts. This apparent absence of violent crime, armed conflict and mental and physical disease can be explained on the basis of instructions which promote creative, rather than destructive, interpersonal relations. Dream helps them to live in harmony with each other. This case is compared to that of the Ngoni people of Malawi, who have occupied part of central Malawi.

Dream among the Senoi

The Senoi people are guided by dreams in all that they do. They all respect dreams. In the morning, according to Noone, they all gather for dream discussion in the 'long-house.' The male population gathers in the council, at which the dreams of older children and all men in the community are reported, discussed and analysed. Every member of the group who dream the night before vigorously relates his experience in emotional detail. These morning inquests are crucial.

The most significant dreams are interpreted by the senior halak* and other elders of the group. Most of their dreams concern the things that lie ahead. In this sense I would say the dreams show them their destiny or their future. These dreams are present as riddles, parables and dramas.[50] They are full of symbols to be deciphered and exploited. The group advise and encourage each other through dreams. Dreams are a form of education. It is through dreams that a child is socialised and indoctrinated into its environment.

It seems to me that male dreams, as opposed to women's, are taken seriously. A man's experience leads him to believe that if you cooperate with goodwill in the daytime, images of that day will eventually help you in your dreams, and that every person should, and can, become the supreme ruler and maker of his own dreams or spiritual universe, and can determine and receive the help and cooperation of all the forces there.

Since men's dreams are taken more seriously than women's, it follows that boys' dreams are also taken more seriously than girls'. Hence at the morning 'inquest' the father listens with deliberately more interest to the dreams of his male children than to those of his female children. This is also reflected in the fact that girls do not become halak, which is the exclusive preoccupation of men. The special interest shown in boys' dreams and their interpretation is therefore really to prepare them for their future roles as halaks.

Sexual experience in dreams is charged with spiritual and ceremonial significance. Permission for marriage is granted from parents once it is reported that a girl and a boy have dreamt of each other.[51] Interestingly enough, they have to be honest in this matter, as it is considered sacred. The Senoi hold that the whole
* Halak: A shaman or medicine man; every adult who is capable of leading a ritualistic dance is in effect a halak.

of nature is impregnated with spirits, some of which are good and some bad. The group keep in touch with the good spirits through the halaks, who makes personal contact with them in their dreams.[52]

The Senoi believe a man has different souls, such as the head soul, which controls the nervous system; the heart soul, which rules the constantly changing rhythms of the body; the liver soul, which is prescient and can step into the future; and the eye soul, which embraces all the sensory functions of the body and helps to express a man's ideas and register his sympathy or other emotions. Of all these souls, the nervous-system soul is believed to be the one that helps the Senoi to control their dreams. The fact that they can remember and relate their dream experiences in the morning shows that they have natural lucid dreams. The Senoi believe there is a soul which controls the nervous system and that their dreams can be controlled and manipulated, too. Holman mentions that Noone also stresses this factor when he says, 'Temiar dreams are manipulated by advice, encouragement and auto-suggestion.'[53]

The Senoi dreaming life is associated with dancing. Dancing is probably related to the heart soul, which rules the constantly changing rhythms of the body. Often a good spirit resembles a monster or takes an animal shape to test the dreamer's strength and courage. Once the dreamer takes the challenge and fights the animal-like good spirit, it becomes his/her 'gunig', or guide spirit. 'Adoption of a "gunig" is the requirement of becoming a halak. It's only after this adoption that one might announce to the group that one had been requested to lead them in a "gensak" or chain pattern dance.[54] Guide spirit gives advice in dreams, telling halaks to fast for a day and abstain from sexual practice until the dance is over. The participants follow a leader in a line while dancing. Sometimes the rhythm goes slow and this helps the body to relax. After half an hour or so, the leader begins to increase the rhythm, until a climax is reached with a burst of speed and shouting.

At this juncture the music stops and the leader and some or all of the dancers collapse and lie writhing or rigid in a catatonic trance on the floor. They are at this stage said to be possessed by the 'gunig' of the leader. In this state a man does not recognize individuals as he wanders about reciting mystical spells in unintelligible spirit talk. But presently, if called upon, he will prophecy or give a blessing. This is also related to what happens in Malawi, where spirit possession, called *malombo*, sends people into a trance and gives them spiritual powers to prophecy. This will be discussed later in the book.

The trance state, as Noone states, is the outward and visible sign of the 'gunig's' approval of the dreamer. By inciting his followers to perform its dance, he has obtained for his spirit guide recognition by the group and therefore prestige in the spirit world. The dreamer now becomes a halak, 'since it is only by attaining a trance that a young man can demonstrate shamanistic power'.[55] Thus, maintaining the spiritual and physical health of the group is the main aim of the dance. Healing and other benefits are bestowed in the semi-trance state.

As stated above, dreaming seems to give the Senoi a sense of direction. It helps them to make their daily decisions and encourages them to live in harmony with each other. This shows us that dream is very useful and quite normal. Marie-Louise von Franz, as quoted by Jane Ferguson, foremost Jungian analyst who is in her mid-seventies and was taught by Jung himself, believes that if we are not connected with our dream life we may develop a neurosis. Attending to our dreams, she believes, is the healthiest thing we can do. Dreams show us our destiny and how to realise the greater potential of life within us.[56] This technical, sophisticated world has lost a great value in dream. Dream is supposed to be analysed and interpreted. It is only after its meaning is known that people can remain in peace. Dream has value and function. It comes to us to encourage us.

The Ngoni of Malawi

Just as the Senoi respect and listen to the dream, the Ngoni of Malawi also take dream seriously. It is very interesting to find some similarities in the dream world of the Senoi of Malaysia and the Ngoni of central Malawi. As with the Senoi, it is customary for the Ngoni children to share their dreams with the adults. Unlike the Senoi, though, Ngoni children's dreams are not taken seriously. Women listen but without enthusiasm.

What normally happens is that when the adults are sharing their dreams in the morning the children are also there listening and they too recall their dream experiences. As more and more people gather, this becomes a big assembly. Unlike the Senoi assembly, the Ngoni's is not pre-arranged and has no routine. Thus, people gather to share their ideas. The gathering is not institutionalised. You don't actually sit down in the morning specially for dreams. But since people, especially women, are fond of sitting outside in the morning to enjoy the sunshine, these gatherings become somewhat patterned and many issues are dis·cussed. They can discuss other issues as well, but dreams just come because it is in the morning, when people have just woken up, fresh with dreams of the previous night.

People in Malawi take education serious. Actual success, or lack of it, is commonly associated with educational attainments. As such, many dreams concern passing or failing exams. In the afternoon, when the children go out, they meet their peers and discuss with their friends their dream experience. If a child dreams he was far in the sky without falling down, their parents would interpret it as an indication that he has passed his exams. If, on the other hand, a child dreams he has been drowning in the water or failing to cross a river, it is interpreted as meaning he has failed his exams. Children sometimes have frightening dreams and scream during the night or look terrified in the morning. For this reason adults always discourage children's dreams. They are not to believe in dreams lest they come true. The pattern of adult dreams, however, differs from that of their children. For instance, when adults dream of crossing a river, it means someone is going to die.

My mother, who is now more than ninety years of age, had a dream in June 1990. She dreamt she was with someone on one side of a river. My father was standing on the opposite side. This other person was telling my mother to cross the river. 'Let's go to that other side,' the man said while pulling a goat in his hand. He was staggering, for the goat was heavy, and he was unable to walk fast. Instead he insisted that my mother should lead the way. My mother could see my father on the other side also calling her. She really wanted to follow him but because there was a storm (mafunde) she failed to cross and later she got up and realised it had only been a dream. The interpretation of her dream was that she could have died if she had crossed to join my father. My father, who was calling her, actually died years ago. To follow a dead person calling you in a dream means certain death.

Although children's dreams are discouraged, experience shows that they mean a lot and would reveal a lot of insights if recorded. While the Senoi teach morality to their children through dreams, the Ngoni also rely on dreams to express the need to maintain high morals. If you offend someone, ancestors will tell you in a dream to go and apologise.

One of my nieces, by the name of Harriet, had a dream while I was in Malawi in August 1990. She was twelve years of age. In her dream, she saw water boiling in big pots, producing a lot of steam. Her mother, my sister Florence, interpreted water boiling as a sign of hell: Harriet would go to hell if she died, and did not change her way of life. Personally I wondered what sorts of sin Harriet could have committed at such a young age. Later I realised it was another way of teaching morality. Parents use dreams as a socialising agent.

There are also some cases where two people can have the same kind of dream. Supposing two people quarrel and are not speaking to each other. Both of them could have a dream each, asking the other to apologise. One lady could take the initiative to go and apologise, seeking reconciliation. When she gets there she finds the other lady also troubled in heart and they share their dream experience. Later you see them becoming even closer friends simply because of the dream. The result of discussing a dream can make or encourage closer relationships.

Adults' dreams are taken, analysed and interpreted seriously. Dreams give them inner confidence which allows them to manipulate them and explore their meanings. They are deeply aware of their dreams. They have natural lucid dreams which they can remember and say they did not know were dreams, but thought they were events taking place during waking life. In some cases they dream in symbols, such as seeing ancestors, or a lion, snake or ghost.

If someone has a bad dream, he looks very sad in the morning and tells the family what is troubling him. The family tries to interpret the dream. If it's a frightening dream they will go to an elderly person who is proficient at interpreting dreams. There is at least one dream diviner in every village. Adults go to this individual to listen to what he/she has to say about that bad dream.

The diviner may advise that villagers to take medicine to sprinkle around their houses so as to prevent the beast seen in the dream from reappearing. These prescriptions are taken so seriously that the entire village is involved in administering the medicine. The similarity is that both the Senoi and the Ngoni need their dreams.

Sometimes a dream can be a premonition. For example, if women have arranged a journey and during the night one dreams that someone drowned when crossing a river, or was involved in a car crash, they would advise each other in the morning not to travel. The daughter of Mai Ndongela, an old lady in our village, arranged to travel from Lizulu to Lilongwe. Mai Ndongela dreamt the bus was going to be involved in an accident and prevented her daughter from travelling. She told her she had had a bad dream the previous night. She saw the bus falling into the river Linthipe. The bridge across the river was very narrow in the 1950s and prone to accidents, particularly involving larger vehicles. The daughter took heed of that warning and did not travel. The bus did indeed have an accident on the bridge and many people lost their lives.

Like the Senoi, there are times when Ngoni girls and boys sometimes dream about their would-be partners. Unlike the Senoi, Ngoni parents intervene to stop a girl from marrying the man in her dreams. In most cases the girl discusses this with her parents if she is determined to marry the man. Interestingly, if it's an adult who had the dream, she will just marry him without any hesitation. This originates from the fact that children's dreams are not taken seriously. Equally it is also believed that an adult is capable of making her own decisions. But with a girl or a boy, adults have to give some guidance.

On the other hand, to dream of a wedding is to have death in the family. In other words, there are dreams which show the opposite of what would happen. If they don't like the man they would say that is the opposite. 'We might even have a death in the family.' On the other hand there are some people who dream the direct thing. Those who dream of an event directly are very much respected, as are those who interpret.

Another similarity between the Senoi and the Ngoni is that of the Omen. If a dream is about a strange beast the dreamer has to take it as an obligation to tell the person in the dream to take care. If he does not and if a bad thing or death happens to him, his own conscience would haunt him. If you don't advise that person after a bad thing happens and you reveal that you had that bad dream, society condemns you. Hence to dream of an owl standing on the roof of a house where someone is very sick definitely means that person is going to die.

Spirit possession

The question of spirits is very complicated. However, it is believed that a person's spirit does not go straight to join those who died before him. It lingers in trees, jungles, grasses, etc. It sometimes returns to the village, especially to haunt other family members. Once a person dies rumours circulate of that person's lingering spirits, which stay with the community for a period of time. People become frightened. Lingering spirits do not really play an intermediary role, since they would have not reached the ancestral stage of the spirit world. To send them away, the deceased family are supposed to purify them before they join the ancestral spirits. It is this time before the purification that the spirits work or create a lot of havoc, e.g. causing illness. They become wanderers.

The spirits which appear in dreams are those of ancestors. They are regarded as pure since they attained the spiritual status while in the grave. They take care of us and convey messages to us through dreams.

Among the Ngoni, if we see a person in a village being sick for quite a long time, it is said that the person is possessed by spirits. These can be good or bad. Good spirits would be those from the ancestral world. Bad spirits would be associated with witches. His family would go to a medicine man or diviner, who would persuade the spirits to leave the bewitched person alone. People get cured this way.

While in Malawi in August 1990, I met Nelson Ligomeka, who has done an extensive study of the spirits. He is currently doing his Masters degree in Religious Studies at Chancellor College, a constituent college of the University of Malawi. He told me of different spirits. In the north of Malawi these are called *vimbuza*. In the lower Shire they are called *malombo* and in the central they are called *mashawi* or *vibanda*. In the south of Malawi they are called *mazinda*. Perhaps I could refer to just one of these, because they all play a similar role. I will look at the *malombo* spirit of

Lower Shire Valley. A person who is possessed by *malombo* suffers for quite a long time. When a diviner is consulted they are told the spirits want to manifest in the patient. The relatives then say words of incarnation. They pour water on to the ground. In this way the spirit is identified. After this ceremony the patient shivers and the eyes turn red. This is followed by dizziness and the patient can run away if not guarded. The spirit then starts speaking and reveals that he is the one who has been causing the sickness.

The spirit then demands beer and a lamb to be offered as sacrifice. A *malombo* dance is organised. While the drums are in motion the lamb is slaughtered and its blood is mixed with *mwabvi*, a herbal medicine, and spilled. The patient is brought to the place where the *mwabvi* has been poured and dances more vigorously to the beat of the drums. This is said to be one way of pleasing the spirits. The person no longer suffers since the spirit has been identified.

They normally have to identify the spirit before giving any medicine, because there are many alien spirits. Ranger and Kimambo in their book *The Historical Study of African Religion*, support the idea of many alien spirits. Their research was conducted in Malawi and other countries. They assert, 'Very large numbers of men and women were held to be possessed by the spirits of 'alien' men, or of animals or divinities, in which there was little control by the religious or secular establishment; and in which the idea of possession and the reality of the trance state was used to 'cure' diseases and neuroses by means of initiation into a spirit cult'.[57] It happens, however, that the spirit can return to demand a *nsembe* (thanksgiving). In that case people plead with the spirit to spare the patient. If they don't give *nsembe* the patient dies. The man who gave me this information told me his own sister had died of spirit possession.

Soul

Although there are many spirits, the Ngoni, unlike the Senoi, believe in one soul. They believe this soul leaves the body during the night, associates with the ancestor and brings messages. They believe a person does not really sleep during the night. She or he knows what is going on. They believe God sends warnings through the ancestors against evil.

Falling in trance

Falling in trance is very common among the Ngoni. A person falls to the ground in fits and talks aloud in strange tongues. It is generally believed that trance is some kind of spirit possession. It is the possessing spirit which speaks, not the person who has fallen in trance. This explains the use of unknown foreign languages in trance mode. The importance of trance, however, is that existing outstanding social problems are revealed. For instance, if people had been plotting against someone, it would come out during this moment. It is therefore an important mediator and trouble-shooter. Some people, after the trance, remember and some do not. When he has finished talking, spirits leave the person temporarily. To get rid of the spirits permanently, a thin porridge is normally prepared at this stage for the sick person. This is administered together with herbal medicines.

The herbal medicine* is very strong and helps a lot. I once fell in a ten hour trance myself when my father was murdered. People took time to attend to me since my father's burial had already taken place. Traditionally, women remain at the bereaved family's home for at least a week to cheer them and help with day-to-day chores. I was away from home when the burial took place. When I reached home I only saw these women and fell in trance. I don't think I spoke to anyone at all. I just reached home and collapsed straight away. I did not know what was happening. In the morning I got up and took a bucket, wanting to go to the well to fetch water. But the women prevented me, saying, 'No, no, don't go to the well, you are not feeling alright.' Others pointed out, 'She is upset, the death has come as a shock.' Our village medicine woman came and prepared porridge for me to eat. They never told me what had happened but I had an idea through the herbal medicine which was given to me. Actually, my mother persistently prevented me from going to the well even months after my trance episode. There was a day I insisted and she told me I was going to drown if I went to the well. With those words I knew what had

---

*I prefer to use the term 'herbal medicine' as opposed to the 'African medicine' as is commonly used in sociological literature on Africa. The use of roots, leaves and herbs in general is not unique to Africa. It is a popular form of medicinal administration in China, India and even Europe. There is therefore no basis for associating herbal medicine with Africa as if it is unique to that continent. In actuality, herbal medicine is the primary source of modern pharmaceuticals.

happened. Funeral-related trances are very common in Malawi, particularly among women.

Mystical power is also present in African villages. It occurs in different forms. In one form the person finds himself in a trance. He reveals certain events which will happen in the future. This may include the death of a prominent man in the village or that of a relative; or the birth of a child by a barren woman. Often at the end of the trance period the person is unable to remember all he had revealed, and denies everything. Yet the listeners are able to narrate his revelations. He appears to have been in a dream but on waking to be unable to remember all that happened in the dream.

This sort of dream also brings a message that the person has been pressed hard by the society and is unable to reveal his problems. He is somehow alienated from the society. Then he falls in a trance and we are in a position to hear all the problems he had. If a diviner is near we call her to come and listen. And one is in a better position to suggest what ought to be done. What they normally do when the person who fell into a trance finishes talking is to prepare porridge and put some herbal medicines for him to eat.

When he is talking like that some people are touched and cry because some of the things she is revealing are the things which were actually said to her by some of them. To this extent the listeners would confess that they did not know they were offending her. After the sickness is over people treat the person who fell in a trance differently or with great respect. Now the society does not want to ill-treat that person again. The society makes the dreamer happy so that she does not repeat it again. This is an example of how dreams have helped shape African society.

As stated at the beginning of this book, as Sutherland puts it Jung sees dreams as expressing archetypal aspects of the dreamer which in his working hours remain largely hidden.[58] R. D. Cartwright in *Night Life* (1977) also states that dreams are drawn from the inner responses to experiences which have received too little attention, either for emotional reasons, as Freud might view it, or simply because that is a more efficient use of time.

Another form is often practised by some traditional herbalists/diviners. While he is in this state he can reveal what had happened in the past as well as what could happen in future. One of the herbalists once told his client, who visited him from another village, how her husband died from poison administered by his own brother. He revealed the time of the day and the year her husband died and where his body was found. Later the husband's brother confessed to the murder.

What a person is rehearsing is what puts him in a state of mind. He can reveal anybody's experiences about the past. This is also used if there is a new child brought to a herbalist to trace his identity. The herbalist in this sense puts himself in a trance. Once he gets out of that ecstatic state he forgets he was in a trance.

A common feature of this form and the previous one is that both the herbalist/diviner and the person who finds himself in a trance confess they thought they were dreaming and could not remember what happened in the dream. It's only the listeners who know what had been said.

This chapter has dealt with lucid natural dreams by the Senoi people of Malaysia and by the Ngoni of Malawi. I have also included other case studies, as in the case of Peter Dowd's dreams. These are termed 'natural lucid dreams', 'Natural' in the sense that they are spontaneous and impromptu. People do not make a prior plan of their dream, as is the case with the laboratory dream. The Senoi have positive dreams which help them to live in harmony with each other. Like the Senoi, the Ngoni of Malawi are also helped by dreams to live in harmony with each other and reconcile their differences.

Chapter 2

The Author's Dream Experience

With illustrations from my own dreams, I will show in this chapter two of the central elements of dreams: prophecy and their universality describing in detail my dream experiences both in Africa, where I grew up as a child, and in Britain, where my dreams were recorded. I'll be drawing upon events which have directly affected my family in general and myself in particular. I will be examining through these case studies the central reality of dreams in man's day-to-day life and how they influence decision-making.

These dreams are grouped into three categories, based on their content and interpretation. Category one carries those dreams concerning dreaming about self. Category two incorporates those dreams where other members of my family take prominence in their interpretation and effects. Category three covers dreams by other people, not necessarily within my own family. To show the commonality of category three-type dreams, I have included a discussion of dreams of an old Sudanese lady who accurately predicted in her dreams the future of another Sudanese girl, Grace Jal-wang, who is now married and living in England. We see in these circumstances similarities in how dreams are perceived and interpreted in different cultural settings.

The principal argument in this chapter is that dreams are dreamt for a reason. it may be to encourage us or to warn us. Since dreams foretell the future, they act as messages from God. The distinction made between natural and sleeping laboratory dreams in Chapter 1 forms the very basis of our argument about the naturalness of the relationship between God and the dreamer and God's intention in appearing in dreams. The point is that induced dreams may come at a time when God is not ready to send a message to the dreamer.

In this case the dreamer may not gain the full benefits of dream messages. This, however, does not necessarily mean that artificial dreams are meaningless, just their meaning can be obscured.

It needs therefore to be acknowledged that, once the subject has been induced into dreaming, there is a chance that God might reveal certain archetypes which are hidden in each individual's conscious mind. The unconscious mind brings a message to the conscious mind. The unconscious, as Jung puts it, acts as the omniconscious or the omniscience.[1] Thus, the usefulness of laboratory dreams cannot completely be denied.

As argued in Chapter 1, there are a number of conflicting schools of thought regarding the origin of dream and their role in man's life. Ann Faraday (1972), who represents the latest stage in dream development from a psychotherapeutic point of view, argues that dreams are a reflection of how the individual sees his world and are sometimes more frank than his waking description would be. Faraday sees dream as a continuity from waking to sleeping.[2] It is also an attempt to reconcile what has not received proper attention during the day. In this way dream plays an important role. Without dream the day's business would remain incomplete. This supports the internalist school of thought which argues that dreams originate from within self.

Whichever school of thought one follows there remains the problem of verification. The dreamer is his/her own witness and it is only the dreamer who can verify the accuracy of a dream and its details.

Dreams in Africa

I had three dream premonitions while young, all of which came to fruition years later. After that I grew up respecting dreams. Indeed, in several cases dreams have served as a guide to me and, more importantly, prophesied impending danger. My dream experience makes me argue that the full realisation of dreams can only emerge from their naturalness of origin. There are three types of dreams prescribed – dreams about self; dreams other family members; and dreams about people generally.

Dreams about self

Dream 1: Positive dreams

I was fond of going to Sunday school while a little girl, and went regularly. I never missed going each Sunday.

One night in 1953, at the age of nine, I dreamt I was going to be an ordained minister. I woke up very excited the following morning and decided to share my dream experience with my mother. 'I dreamed I was in the pulpit in the church, preaching. I was dressed in a black gown with a white collar,' I said, becoming very excited. 'Are you mad to think you could be a church minister!' My mother exclaimed! 'Where on earth have you ever seen a woman minister?' she enquired with a mixture of disapproval and bewilderment.

My mother was a very strict disciplinarian and a highly conservative Christian. She was brought up in the confines of orthodox religious teachings of the Scottish church, she was generally opposed to anything that contradicted these teachings. To her, religious teachings were God-given and therefore sacred holy ground not to be tampered with. As an individual she is reserved and very economical with words. She would not like to question divinity. I could see in my mother's eyes that she was not at all amused by my dream. Historically, the Presbyterians, like most Christian churches, have been against women priests. It was therefore very unusual to my mother even to hear that a girl should dream of becoming a church minister.

By contrast, my father listened to my dreams with great enthusiasm. he suggested to my mother that she should not be too hard with me, arguing that it was, after all, only a dream. he even rhetorically suggested that things would change in future. 'Women might be allowed into the ministry of God,' he pointed out emphatically.

What was remarkable about my father's position in this exchange was his allusion to the fact that women may one day be allowed into the ministry of God. My father had liberal ideas which set him far ahead of his time. This probably explains the action that he later took to break away from the Presbyterian church and establish his own church which embraced both African culture and modern religious ideologies.

Fifteen years later, my dream was realised. I was admitted into Nkhoma theological college. This was, however, not without opposition. My admission created deep divisions within the church. There was, on the one hand, a group of elderly conservative church ministers who were totally opposed to any relaxation of the rules of admission of women into theology. They therefore both overtly and covertly campaigned for my removal from the college. On the other hand, there was a group of young-to-middle-aged 'enlightened liberal' church ministers who supported the ordaining of female priests. This was the group that strongly supported my admission and helped to see me through the course. After graduating I took up a position with the church as a religious instructor in secondary schools.

There was yet another dimension to this debate, which erupted after I had finished my course. While it was not vehemently polemical to train female theologians, it was uncompromisingly controversial to see such female theologians preach. Indeed, the conservative priests yielded to the liberal ministers only on the understanding, that no female theologians were to be allowed to preach but would be given other clerical duties. I was once asked by Revd. Mulenga to preach during Easter. Afterwards a row erupted among the church ministers and elders. But the position the church took *vis-à-vis* my Easter sermon was for me the climax of the whole dream interpretation process that I had started fifteen years earlier. This was the realisation of the dream.

From the foregoing, regardless of whether or not dream is a wish-fulfilment, it is arguable that dreams do predict the future. They are prophetic and the fact that they are realised is an affirmation of that truism. It can also be argued that dreams carry with them a strong sense of predestination. The point is that, when I was being considered for theological admission, other girls had also applied for entry. While my application had aroused the interest of the 'liberal' group, they did not find it possible to support other female applications. Thus, in the context of my thesis, there was a reserved place for me to occupy, a place I understand as having been reserved by God, in fulfilment of the promise He had made in my dream fifteen years earlier.

This argument can also be constructed from the perspective of the general unprecedent enthusiasm with which some members of the church dedicated their time and financial resources to expedite my stay in college. For example, they offered to take over my responsibilities to my extended family. Both the Moderator and the General Secretary of the church promised to pay school fees for my nieces and nephews, who were going to be deprived of my financial support by my having taken up theological studies. The church also offered to console my mother, who was paranoid about my whole venture into the 'men's world'.

Dream 2: Negative prophecy: inescapable tragedy

In 1954 I had another vivid dream experience. I dreamt that I was beaten to the point of death. I shared this dream with my mother. She kept quiet, offering no comment. After the first encounter with my father in 1953, instead of dismissing me outright she was inclined to give more serious thought to the implications of my other traumatic dreams. In response, therefore, she enforced restrictions on my movements. I was not allowed to move about. I was kept at home. I could not go to the well to draw water, nor go to the market.

On one summer holiday one of my friends who had been with me in primary school came to visit me. It was on a Saturday afternoon. I had not seen this girl since we left primary school. We were naturally excited and talked about all the little things we did together in school including *masanje*. We stayed the whole afternoon chatting. At about 5 p.m. she started back to her village. Traditionally, it is courteous to escort one's visitor home, though not obligatory. My mother prevented me from escorting her, but my sisters pleaded with her to let me go. She yielded and allowed me to take my friend to the main road, which was fifty yards away from our house. I was pushing my friend's bike.

When we reached the main road a stoutly built man joined us. He picked up our conversation and asked what we were talking about. My friend thought that our conversation was none of this strange man's business and told him so. A row started. I kept quiet since I did not want to be involved. Surprisingly, the man simply chased my friend away and turned back, saying it was me that he really wanted. It did not occur to me to run home at the time he was pursuing my friend. I stood there as if I was possessed or mesmerised. Besides, I was holding my friend's bike, which made it a bit awkward to run.

However, the point is that the man came back and kicked me hard. On seeing this my friend bravely went around calling people to come to my rescue. Surprisingly, although people ran to the scene, none of them challenged this man. They all stood there watching as if it were a bullfight. To them it was like watching a drama. After beating me for what felt like forty-five minutes, a certain man Mr Mulangeni, who had been my father's good friend, came running to rescue me. He managed to save my life. By then I was bleeding profusely. Blood was oozing from my mouth, nostrils and other parts of the body. Incidentally, this was the very same spot where my father had been killed in 1963.

Meanwhile, my family had prepared their evening dinner and they were all eating except my mother. She was very worried why it was taking me so long to return home and wondered what had happened. My sister tried to persuade her to eat. She refused. 'Mary does not go anywhere. Something must have happened,' she said. My sister suggested that probably we had reached my friend's place and that her brother was going to escort me back. My mother was unconvinced. She decided to wait for me and eat after I had returned.

All of a sudden my friend appeared, breathless, at the door. Seeing her all by herself, my mother sensed something was wrong. 'Mary has been killed,' my friend announced. They all rushed to the scene. All my sisters and my nieces had come. I was aware of their presence but somehow I was unable to communicate that I was alive. It was all dark and I could not see anything. I could hear them crying and was able to recognise their voices, but I felt numb and powerless to do anything.

A white Portuguese man who was also a good friend of my father suggested taking me to the hospital. But people told him not to bother since they reckoned I was already dead. He insisted however. He first took me to a mission hospital called Mlanda. a The doctor there refused to admit me, saying I was already dead. My escort did not lose heart. Instead he took me to a government hospital at Dedza *boma*/(medical centre), where I was immediately admitted. The following morning I opened my eyes round about eleven o'clock. My mother could not believe it. She sat by my bedside. It was a relief to her. She had not thought I would regain consciousness.

With this dream I learned that one cannot escape dream predictions. I tried to be indoors, but it was all in vain. The tragedy had to be fulfilled. Dudley (1969), in his book *Dreams – Their Mysteries Revealed*, was confronted with the same problem. He argues that if the future can be predicted in dreams, then in some comprehensible way it must already exist.[3] It seems to me that the predicted incident is already there waiting for you. Our unconscious mind illuminates that future. In this way the unconscious is ahead of the conscious mind.

If that is a correct interpretation, then there is no freewill. One's future is pre-planned and awaits one's day-to-day living, which only fulfils this godly plan. Thus dream messages are inescapable. The only condition that reverses dream predictions is when in the same dream you are instructed to take certain counter-measures. We will explore this theme later in other dreams.

Dreaming about other members of the family

Dream 3: Tragedy (My father's death)

This dream came before dream 2, but was in the same year, 1953. I dreamt once that my father had been beaten by some unknown people and left lying dead by the roadside. In the dream I had a vivid picture of the 'battle' scene between my father and his assassins. As usual I shared the dream with my mother. Out of fear of the unknown I even suggested to her that we move away from that place and settle somewhere else. As mentioned in Chapter 1, children's dreams are not take seriously among the Ngoni. For this reason, and since it was also her characteristic, she just expelled me and thought something was wrong with me. She did not pay any attention. My father, on the other hand, listened carefully and tried to reason with my mother once again that she should not just be ignoring my dreams. He argued that some people are gifted and what they dream becomes true.

To console me, my father pointed out that we would have moved somewhere, but there was no money for such a move. For this reason we stayed at Lizulu. Ten years hence my father was actually beaten to the point of death. He was taken to the nearby mission hospital called Mlanda, only for the doctor to tell the family that he had stopped breathing on his way to the hospital. The doctor could not do anything but pronounce death.

I was in a boarding secondary school when this was taking place. I did not come to know about it until a week or so later, when I met a girl who asked me whether I had been home. I told her I hadn't. She therefore narrated the story of my father's death. I immediately had a flashback of my dream discussion with my parents ten years before. Here was yet another confirmation of the power of dreams. 'So I was right,' I said to myself.

With much thought regarding this incident, I came to believe that dream is not just a meaningless adventure into the unconscious world, nor is it 'without meaning' as Peter Medawar puts it.[4] Dream has future connotations. As Jung stated, 'Dream expresses archetypal aspects of the dreamer which in his waking hours remain largely hidden.'[5] I was young when I had this dream and I did not have any idea of death. It didn't even occur to me that people kill each other. In other words, I did not know what killing meant. The dream brought a message which I was not consciously aware of.

Certainly, we see in these two related dreams the power of dreams. Dreams grab us, affect us and involve us.[6] They give a warning about future events. In this sense Francis Crick, as has already been referred to in Chapter 1, is right in pointing out that dreams foretell the future, while von Franz, as quoted by Jane Ferguson in the *Guardian* of 26 April 1989, insists that dreams never tell us what we already know. There are external forces which are continuously at work on us. Dreams are messages from God.[7] We can argue that the dreams described above were warning dreams and that they came from God. But to argue in this case that my father's death would have been prevented by moving elsewhere would be stretching our logic a bit too far and we will leave that to conjecture and for readers to interpret. But what is important in this dream is that everything that might have prevented the tragedy was rendered ineffectual by financial constraints. I have to repeat here that it is customary in African dream not to question what has been said in dream, meaning if the need to change homes was part of the dream, my parents would have conceded. They did not take action because the request came from me purely out of fear of the unknown.

True, there are some dreams which are difficult to understand

and to interpret. But if we analyse them critically we do get the answer in the end. Jung sees them falling into some kind of mathematical equation; we cannot say to what physical realities they correspond. So in the case of some mythological products we do not know at first to what psychic realities they refer. Jung further asserts that it is only when we let its statements amplify themselves, that it comes within the range of our understanding. Only then does a new aspect become perceptable to us.[8] In fact it could be argued that only a dreamer can understand his own dream. This is the reason why we dream about our families and friends. It is also easy to interpret a dream of a person whom you know very well, and again if you know his or her acquaintances.

The three dreams described above were the most vivid ones I had while young. They left an indelible mark on my memory, so much so that I will never question as to what a dream is. I just took a dream as a natural and a normal thing. In those days, everywhere I went with my peer group, we were busy sharing and interpreting dream. If the dream was unusual we could consult the elderly. Dream interpretation became a habit to us.

Dream 4: Dream about sister's death: prior fears

It was in 1973 that I encountered yet another forewarning dream. I dreamt that my sister had died. I shared this dream with one of my friends I was staying with in Lilongwe, Malawi. My friend had a car. We then decided to drive to my home district, Ntcheu, to see if my sister was alright. When we reached home we found she was alive but very sick. She had cancer of the uterus and by then the doctor had already decided that there was no hope, since it had already spread to the whole body. He would have operated on her if we had taken her to the hospital much earlier. I told my mother why we had come. Remember at this time the dreams I had while a little girl had already happened. With this in mind, my mother kept quiet. Apparently that quietness meant agreeing with the dream. However, my friend and I returned to Lilongwe. The following week my sister died.

Although it is arguable here that the dream was a confirmation of my own fears, since I knew my sister had cancer, the question still remains, why should the dream occur to me and not any other members of the family? They were just as worried as I was at the time. Consequently, I would like to believe that dreams still carry messages of their own to inform us of what lies ahead.

As I have stated, the dream about my sister's death was useful. It was useful in the sense that I did not travel anywhere outside Lilongwe. I waited patiently at my house until the following week the message reached me. It was useful because the news did not come to me as a shock. It was something which the dream had already told me. Whether it was from God or not, the dream gave a warning message; it was a natural lucid dream. There are several characteristics which seem to provoke natural lucidity. More importantly, anxiety since the doctor had already told us her chances of survival were slim. In this context the usefulness of dreams could be seen with the aid of the understanding of our conscious mind. It could be seen, then, that the internalist school of thought, which argues that dreams originate from within self, is also plausible.

Dreams, in my mind, do appear to us for a reason. Jung was of the opinion that 'the dream does not conceal. We simply do not understand the language'. He said further, 'Dreams are as simple or as complicated as the dreamer is himself. Only they are a little bit ahead of the dreamer's consciousness.'[9] It is true dreams are ahead of us. They tell us something which may be unacceptable in our present frame of thinking and we may therefore dismiss them as madness or illogical or irrational. Yet when it comes to pass we look back and think of what message the dream was bringing to us.

Dreams in Britain

Dream 1: Nakedness dream

Sometimes a dream tells me what I am going to do the following morning. I was working at a home for the physically handicapped when I had this dream. At first the dream did not really impress me and I thought of not recording it. But when it happened I started paying attention and asked myself why should dreams be telling me about these things? Having examined it, I came to the conclusion that the dream was not meaningless, it carried a message of its own.

In the dream I saw one of the residents by the name of Fred Mitchell, sleeping naked in his own bed in his room. I said to him, 'Why are you sleeping naked? Can't you use your blankets?' 'No,' he replied. I tried to reason with him to use at least his pyjamas. He still refused. He did not want them. He was happy sleeping like that. I left him and said to myself there is no point in arguing with him. I found the dream very unusual and shameful.

It was around 4 a.m. when I had this dream. I went off to sleep again. At 6 a.m. I got up and started getting ready to go to work. Upon arrival at work, I discovered that there were no male staff to attend to the male residents and we were accordingly asked to take charge. I ended up attending Fred Mitchell. Immediately it sparked fresh memories of the dream that I had had a few hours earlier. I found the dream very interesting and shared it with my colleagues during breakfast-time.

I realised the dream was forewarning me of what I was going to do in the next few hours. This is somewhat different from my earlier dreams in terms of the time between a dream and its realisation. This is what I would call 'instantaneous realisation'. It also ties in with Jung's claim that dreams express archetypal aspects of the dreamer which in his waking hours remain largely hidden. I did not know during the previous day that I was going to attend Fred the following day. The interpretation would certainly have been different if, for example, the absentee male nurse had been sick the previous day or had sought permission for leave. But he had not. There was no prior knowledge that on particular morning that he was not coming.

Equally, I did not choose of my own accord to go to Fred in order to fulfil my dream. It just happened that my workmates had already selected their residents to attend. Fred was the only one left. This, in Freud's words, represented a 'royal road' to the unconscious parts of the mind which had hitherto been inaccessible in my search for self-knowledge.[10]

This was precisely the reason why Freud was slowly led to consider that repressed wishes in the unconscious mind found substitute gratification during waking life in the form of dreams. Hence, he never wholly abandoned the idea that dream is a kind of neurotic symptom in its own right.

In this dream the 'wish-fulfilment' interpretation is ruled out since wish-fulfilment has the connotation of prior knowledge.

Rather, it is a kind of 'neurotic symptom'. Moreover, the notion of the dream as natural and as serving a useful function is securely in this dream.

Dream 2: A hole on my right leg

It was on 5 July 1990 that I had another vivid, silly dream. The dream was in the morning at about 7 a.m. I dreamed there was a hole on my right leg.

I was frightened, thinking I had injured myself.

I woke up, prepared to go to work. I decided to wear some new tights which I had just bought. I had a 'networking' meeting to attend that morning at Sefton General Hospital. I went with my line manager, Phil Purvis.

While we were in that discussion group I saw this round hole on my tights. This did not shock me since the dream had already forewarned me. However, I found it fascinating and could not resist showing my colleagues, and we all had a laugh. The motive behind showing them was to tell them about the dream I had had. But then an idea came to me not to tell them since we were busy discussing other issues. It follows, then, that dream is not just about the future but about the present as well. Nevertheless, it could still be argued that it is about the future since it was the dream which came first. All my dreams have been very useful because they all refer to the future. Dudley, as referred to earlier, also wrote on the same issue: 'We are entitled to infer that those dreams which appear to predict the future have greater value than those which fail to predict it.'[11]

A recurring dream about my mother's death

There will be times when some dreams will recur during sleep. They may be pleasant or they may be disturbing.[12] Whatever form they take my experience shows that the dream wants you to take action.

Dream 3

I was working at a home for the physically handicapped when I had this dream. I dreamt that my mother had died. But what was confusing in the dream was the fact that she appeared half dead and half alive where she had lain. Since I was together with my workmates I told them I was going upstairs to turn over my mother. They insisted on coming to help me. But I refused their offer. All the girls went back except Moreen Smith, who persisted in following me. Realising that I was adamant and was not going to allow her in, Moreen forced her way into the room where my mother was lying. I gave up and decided to cooperate. I told Moreen to hold one side of the blanket. When we took off the blankets, we discovered it was not my mother. It was a white man. Moreen jumped. Nevertheless, we went ahead preparing the body for the funeral house. The dream was very strange. – Although the person was a white man, I could still see the features of my mother.

The next morning I went to work. Interestingly, I was told Moreen was not reporting for duty that day because her grandfather was very ill at home and she had to attend to him. I quickly related Moreen's absence to my dream. Unfortunately one week did not elapse before Moreen's grandfather died.

Dream 4: another dream on my mother's death

I had yet another dream concerning my mother's death on 7 October 1989. The dream took much longer than usual. Probably this is the longest dream I have ever had. It almost dominated the whole night. We were driving a car which belonged to one of the girls at my place of work, Lorrain Yates. We were driving along a road passing through thick forests, valleys, hills, passes and along river banks.

The interesting thing was that I kept on changing cars. Sometimes I would be driven by people from home and on other occasions I was in Lorraine's car. The other important part of the dream was that it was difficult for us to reach the funeral home. The passage leading to the coffin was very crowded. Realising we were not going to get anywhere by car I decided to get out and walk. When I reached the place I noticed there was a general excitement in the crowd. Each one of them was trying to direct me. before I was finally there I saw a lot of English children. They had come to attend the funeral. The children looked like the 'Brownies' in our church, the United Reformed (URC). They put on brown uniforms and blue uniforms. Those who had brown uniforms put on blue ties and hats. They were with some teachers who were directing them which way to go. The children looked like a confused flock. My mother's coffin was decorated with red cloth and red flowers.

I asked some people from home the best way to reach the body. Surprisingly, they prevented me from getting near it. I could, however, see the beautifully decorated bed. Nevertheless, some people within the group tried to squeeze me through. They lifted me up. I was then able to reach the top. Even then I did not touch the coffin. Upon reaching the top I discovered to my relief that after all she was only asleep. She had asked to see my two nephews, Zione and Nditani, whom she had actually lived with and was fond of.

Although she had not asked to see me, she was pleased that I had come. 'Is it you, Mary?' she muttered, grabbing my hand. 'It's good you have come. I really longed to see you.'

I woke up in total confusion and asked myself what it all meant, dreaming about 'Brownies' and crowds of millions of English men and women in a Malawian village setting. What was the connection between 'Brownie' and my mother in that beautifully decorated bed as if we were celebrating something? What were we celebrating? Was it the death of a prominent person? Why did she appear dead and at the same time talk to me? Was it just her spirit talking to me, as is the case in African beliefs that the dead can communicate with the living (as we will show in Chapter 3)?

The following morning was a Sunday. I went to church. I belong to the Presbyterian church but I do not really mind which church I go to. URC is a combination of both Presbyterian and other evangelical churches.

All the children I saw in the dream were there. Some had brown jackets with blue ties. Others wore blue uniforms, in total replication of my dream. It was Harvest Sunday and the children were presenting their gifts to their church minister. Although the procession was orderly it was evident that the children were sometimes unsure as to which direction to go. They had to be constantly guided by their teachers.

I immediately remembered the dream. Some might argue that I had prior knowledge of the social setting of the dream and I knew the subjects as members of the church and that the dream was a reflection of the memory I had in my conscious mind. There may be an element of truth in that argument. But the point is that there had been a time-lag between the last time I attended service and the dream. In which case I did not have, in a strict sense, prior knowledge of the rehearsals that had taken place in preparation for this particular Harvest Sunday.

Dream 5: Third dream on my mother's death

Not long after dream 4 I encountered another dream, on 27 October 1989, at about 7.20 a.m. I dreamt that my mother had once again died. I saw her skeleton standing in front of me. The confusing element of this dream was its setting. It seemed as if my mother was in Britain, which made funeral and transportation arrangements difficult. I complained to my brother that I did not have enough money to transport the body home.

I had these three recurring dreams about my mother's death in the same year. An examination could probably be sought from the fact that my mother is ninety years of age. My constant fears about her death and being so far away from Britain sparked these reflections of death.

That these three dreams were repeated could be interpreted to mean that I was being invited to go and see her. As indicated earlier, my mother is very old and I had not seen her for years. As the last-born in the family, it's just as well that she was anxious to see me. Thus, I made an effort to go home. After this trip the dreams never recurred.

While at home I shared my dreams with some elderly diviners, who interpreted them to mean that my mother was going to live long. I told my sister about this and she confirmed it, indicating that my mother had actually been examined by Dr Brinol at Mlanda hospital, the time she was sick and the doctor hinted she had looked after herself very well during her prime age and that she was indeed going to live long.

Dream 6: immediate family: my brother on marrying his own wife

A wedding is normally interpreted at home to indicate a funeral in the family or in a village. It may also mean poverty or loss of money in the family and the dream I am about to narrate illustrates these points.

It was 7 a.m. on 20 April 1990 when I dreamt about my brother's wedding. My brother was actually already married. He had had his wedding several years back. The dream, however, was indicating that he was marrying the same wife. My mother was standing beside them as chief bridesmaid. Interestingly Rita Cosgrove, a second Officer-in-Charge at Parkside hostel, in Liverpool, was also present. I wondered why and how Rita could possibly have travelled to Malawi to attend my brother's wedding. How did she know he was getting married? All these questions were troubling my mind during the dream.

The background to this dream, however, is that when I went home, in August 1990, I heard my brother's marriage was on the rocks and that they were about to divorce. In October 1990 my sister wrote to say that they were separating. But there was also another element of loss of money on the trip when I visited home. I found the family in need of money. I came back to England and borrowed money from my Barclaycard and sent the money home. Then other problems just piled on top of each other. I said to myself, 'What a year is this one?' I have never lost money like the year 1990. Sometimes I wanted to cry; I wondered why this has happened. Gustavus Hindman Miller wrote: 'To attend a wedding in your dream, you will speedily find that there is approaching you an occasion which will cause bitterness and delayed success.'[12]

Miller's interpretation was vindicated in other episodes in my life. I wanted to buy a house and kept enough money for the deposit, but I ended up using all that money due to family problems and the journey I made visiting home. The loss of money sort of delayed success.

There is also another side to the story. I have two brothers. The second brother, whom we did not expect to marry, abruptly changed his mind and married at the age of forty-eight. He married the same year I had the dream. I had the dream in April and my brother got married in December. Although this particular brother was not the central subject of my dream, his wedding was probably the one being predicted.

Dreaming about other people

Dreaming about Mrs Thatcher

On 27 January 1990, at 6.30 a.m. I dreamt Mrs Thatcher was no longer the Prime Minister of the United Kingdom. The word used in the dream was 'sacked.' Big words were also written on the wall in inverted comas: 'MRS THATCHER NO LONGER PRIME MINISTER "SACKED".' There were, however, two people in front of me – Mrs Thatcher and Mr Heseltine, standing on a platform. To their right, at the very end of the platform, was another man whom I did not fully recognise but who looked like Mr Tebbit. Mrs Thatcher was in a blue suit, the one she was fond of wearing when she became Prime Minister. Mr Heseltine was wearing a grey suit. He said to Mrs Thatcher, 'Go away, go away, we are fed up with you.' Mrs Thatcher did not say anything. She started walking away quietly. The moment Mrs Thatcher left the platform the other man, who looked like Mr Tebbit, also left the platform and went to meet Mrs Thatcher. They were talking to each other. Mr Heseltine was left by himself on the platform. Mr Tebbit wanted to show that he was not siding with Mr Heseltine.

I thought this was real. I woke up and recorded the dream and rushed to switch on the radio but there was nothing on the news. I immediately narrated my dream to Charles and Angela Kafumba. Charles is at the moment doing a PhD in economics at Liverpool University. I also shared it with some colleagues at Parkside. One of them, Barbara Lee, corrected me on electoral procedures and said, 'It does not go like that, Mary: no one within the Conservatives can take over. It has to be someone from the Labour Party.' I said to her, 'This is only a dream and I am sharing with you my experience.' I also shared the dream with my neighbours Monica Waterman, who is a sister at the Royal Liverpool Hospital, and her friend. Monica asked, 'Do you mean a Conservative is going to win again? Go away with your dream.' I also related the dream to Pat Bryden, a college lecturer and Mrs Evelyn Jones, who was a missionary in Malawi. Brian Ragbourn, who is currently doing research in Southern African oral tradition, Grace Jal-wang, another friend of mine. I also shared it with Sandra St Rose. Sandra got excited about the dream and said to Martha Igbinovia, 'listen to the dream she had.' Melanie Khan, another friend of mine, who lives in London, was one of the people with whom I shared the dream. She made no comment, but listened with great interest.

I interpreted the dream to mean that Mr Heseltine, since he was left on the platform by himself, was going to be the Prime Minister in future, or the other man who was standing there. But Stan Ruddock, who is in his seventies, with whom I also shared the dream, said the fact that Mr Heseltine was left on the platform did not mean that he would be Prime Minister. His role could be just to get rid of Mrs Thatcher, an interpretation which turned out to be true after the Heseltine leadership challenge. However, Mrs Thatcher resigned of her own accord on 22 November 1990. Just as she had walked willingly from the platform in my dream so she resigned.

The above account is an example of a lucid natural dream. The dream came of its own accord. But the fact is it foretold the future of a leadership contest in Britain which saw the Hon. John Major taking over as Prime Minister from Mrs Thatcher.

I met great opposition concerning the Mrs Thatcher dream; I feel the West has lost the value of dreams. If it had been in Africa, what happened to Mrs Thatcher would not have happened. It would definitely have been prevented, because Mrs Thatcher would have been told by MPs. The MPs on her side would have told her to change her policies. They would have called different diviners to see whether they all interpreted it to mean the same. The dream would have troubled the MPs on Mrs Thatcher's side. They would have told her anyway, while here I became a laughing-stock. However, I am strongly convinced that this would have been prevented.

When it happened some of my colleagues phoned me saying, what sort of dream did you have? Everything you told us has come true. Melanie Khan, who kept quiet on hearing the dream, was the first person to ring me. She said Mrs Thatcher was in a blue suit at the time she resigned. This is amazing. On the other hand some English people to whom I have told the dream pointed out that I said Mr Heseltine was going to become Prime Minister.

They were trying to find faults in the dream, which shows that dreams are not valued much in the West. There were a few exceptions, of course. For example, Pat Bryden, Barbara Lee and Mrs Evelyn Jones all said the dream has taken place.

Those who argued against my dream failed to see the main characters in the dream. Someone who looked like Mr Tebbit was standing aside and followed Mrs Thatcher and they had a long discussion. He was sort of encouraging Mrs Thatcher. Some people who know told me that all through Mr Tebbit sided with Mrs Thatcher. The whole dream was about two people, Mrs Thatcher and Mr Heseltine. And I repeatedly said someone within the Conservative Party would take over. After the incident had happened someone interpreted the dream to mean probably the man whom I could not really identify was Mr Major. That it has happened before finishing writing my book has given me chance to comment. I still maintain that the dream was about Mrs Thatcher and Mr Heseltine only. The dream was even right, because it told me of someone within the Conservatives taking over, because this is also what some people to whom I told my dream argued that I did not know. It does not follow that one can be succeeded by someone within the same party. To end the matter I would say the dreamer is the best interpreter and I still maintain that the dream was a warning dream to reveal beforehand what was going to happen to Mrs Thatcher.

Dream 2: A friend's imprisonment

I had an awful dream. On the morning of 21 July 1990 at 06.05 I dreamt one of my friends was in prison. She was preparing to go to her own country. She had already bought an air ticket. I told her of the dream and she went to negotiate to see if she could get a refund, but the travel agency refused. She had no choice but to go to her country, since she did not want to lose her money for nothing. In early August she went home and she shared my dream with her parents. Nothing happened to her. She had no problems with the police or immigration.

The following week her brother also set off for home. He did not reach it. He was seized at the airport and put in prison. That was a real disaster. My friend's holiday had finished and she had to return to Britain. In this case, although the dream was centred on my friend, I was in fact dreaming about her brother. When you dream of one particular member of a family, it can really be about anyone within that family.

The dream above actually predicted the future. Those who ask can dreams come true can find the answer to most of my dreams. A friend of mine, Sister Alma Binder, from Washington, doubted very much the use of dreams. Although she doubts, her grandmother used to dream and they would make fun of her each time she told them of her dream experiences. Most of her dreams were about a snake and each time she dreamt of a snake there would be a funeral in their family. Thus, although they used to laugh at her, the dreams were to some extent forewarning them of these deaths in the family. However, even though her grandmother's dreams predicted the future, Alma Binder did not believe dreams could be a subject on which to write a book. The coincidence between the grandmother's dreams and the death pattern – led her to change her mind. She later told me that dreaming of a snake definitely means a death in the family.

According to *The Dictionary of Dreams*, by Gustavus Miller Hindman (1983), to dream of a snake is indicative of evil in its various forms and stages. For a woman to hypnotise a snake denotes her rights would be assailed but she would be protected by law and influential friends.[13]

We, however, see two things here: a person whose family is guided by dreams to warn them about future events but still takes the grandmother as a laughing-stock; and a person, despite her grandmother's dream prediction, still ignoring the messages – she needed to open her eyes and accommodate the dream.

However, despite this refusal to acknowledge it the realities of the dream come to pass. The funeral actually occurs. This reminds me of what Brian Inglis wrote in the *Guardian*, 9 September 1987, that even the hundreds of rationalists cannot deny the existence of dreams.

There was yet another friend, Mrs Margaret Chikhadzula. She came over to Glasgow to study for her Master's degree in accountancy. We used to share our dreams while young. She came to visit me in Liverpool during the holiday. I started discussing dreams. She told me that dreams are the work of the devil. When she returned to Glasgow to finish her final year she wrote a letter telling me of a dream she had had. I observed that with great interest. Her dream will be included in Chapter 7 since it is on 'problem-solving.'

Other dreams (intermediaries)

In most cases dreams are thought to be for the dreamer only but it is not always so. Sometimes dreams can be beneficial for other people besides the dreamer or members of his family. In the following cases I will be examining the role of external intermediaries in dreams. By external I mean members outside the dreamer's immediate family. I will discuss dreams from Sudan and Malawi.

An old lady dreaming for Grace Jal-wang

Grace Jal-wang is from Sudan. I was studying with her husband at Liverpool University. I came to know Grace as well. Unlike me she does not take particular pains to remember details of her dreams. She has, however, had a number of interesting dream experience, some of which she has shared with me. She has dreamt about travelling to distant lands, and flying and walking in valleys, green pastures and mountains. She admits that, while she finds these dreams confusing, she believes they have a powerful message for her and probably for other people as well. She actually had a number of dreams in which other people predicted her future; two of these are described below.

An old lady predicts Grace's marriage

One Sudanese lady who was very close to Grace's family and an expert in dreams dreamt that Grace was going to marry a man outside her tribe; Grace received this with contempt. She did not want to accept the idea of marrying someone from a different tribe. According to the Sudanese custom, most people are vehemently opposed to the idea of their daughters marrying men of other tribes or clans. This is mainly a protective mechanism for the preservation of culture and tradition. They hedge against cultural clashes. For example, in Grace's tribe *lobola*, or bride-price, is a normal and acceptable practice and is payable in monetary terms (cash). On the other hand, in her present husband's tribe, while *lobola* is acceptable, cash is not the preferred medium of exchange. Preferable is payment in cattle; 100–150 cows would be an average bride-price, the actual number being directly proportionate to the family definition of their daughter's beauty and education. Grace's contemptuous position in this matter was a reflection of this tribal rejection of inter-cultural marriages. She did not see her family accepting it, so there was therefore no need to even think about it: such a move would be interpreted as rebellious.

However, as the lady predicted in her dream, Grace actually did marry an 'outsider.' She told her husband she knew she was going to marry someone from a different tribe. The interesting thing is that before she got married to her husband she had a fiancé from her own tribe. Everything was arranged, but while they were in the process of getting married Grace saw her fiancé flirting. One day she actually met him with the girl everyone talked about in her village. Grace did not hesitate but called the marriage arrangements off.

Within a few days, Grace met John, her present husband, and exchanged marriage vows. In this case it was a dream come true. The old lady had actually predicted Grace's future and her marriage with John was a fulfilment of that destiny. Von Franz, as mentioned earlier, believes dreams show us how to find meaning in our lives, how to fulfil our destiny, how to realise the greater potential of life. I would not be wrong to say Grace found her confidence in this marriage, since the marriage was predicted.

Dreaming of Grace having three children

Immediately after their marriage, the same lady dreamt about Grace with three girls standing near her. The lady interpreted those three girls as denoting Grace's children. This is consistent with Montague Ullman *et al.*, who argue that in our sleep we have no choice but to attend to the pictures that appear before us and involve us in action. Once awake, we have the option of attending or not attending to the memory of these nocturnal images.[14] Grace has three children and all three are girls, Jackie, Julie and Jane.

Dreams shed light on both the strengths and weaknesses of our emotional healing. That is our relationships with other people. It is different from the physiological in that it takes place in interaction with others rather than within the confines of our own skin.

It is just as real and equally important. Emotions register the state of our relations with others. In fact we dream mainly of the people whom we know very well. One can also dream of an event which is going to happen in the society as has already been discussed earlier in this chapter, even if she is not familiar with them, but only on very rare cases.

Dreaming about Grace going to Britain

Grace's grandfather also had a prophetic dream about Grace's future. He once dreamt, while Grace was in Sudan in her early teens, that she was going to travel to Britain and live there for a long time. Grace's grandpa was worried that he was going to die in her absence. Grace found this dream odd and hard to believe. She wondered how on earth this was going to happen. She did not have any relatives in Britain, neither did she have the means to make the trip. She had yet another worry. If she was to go to Britain all by herself, how was she going to communicate since she only spoke and wrote in Arabic? While pondering these issues she thought of leaving everything in the hands of God. Yet although she left things as they were, she looked forward to travelling to Britain.

As the grandfather predicted, Grace actually made the journey to England with her family, where she is at the present moment. She is very fluent in English and that is not a bother to her any more. It was easy for her to learn English since she was an Arabic teacher. She had the skills of learning. Her grandfather is now dead. He predicted in the dream that Grace was not going to find him.

Dreaming of the author going to Britain

One of my schoolmates, Mwajuma Jaward, while we were in Form 1 in 1963, dreamt I was going to travel to Britain. Although I am a dreamer myself I did not take her dream seriously. Like Grace, I wondered about the logistics of such a journey and thought it was beyond my reach. The same questions were asked to whom I was going to go? What of communication?

However, while I was studying women's leadership in Zambia at Mindolo Ecumenical Foundation the college arranged for me to go to Vancouver, in Canada. I wrote home to the general Secretary, Revd. Chienda, about this. In response, Revd. Chienda asked me to go to Malawi first. While in Malawi I realised that another journey had been arranged for me to go to Britain. It was on this occasion that I remembered what Mwajuma had dreamt about me years back. Her dream foretold my future. In 1977 I travelled to Britain.

We learn in these two dreams the universality of dreams. Jane Ferguson also stated in the *Guardian* (26 April 1989) that Marie-Louise von Franz, the foremost Jungian analyst, believes dreams are universal and that we do dream sometimes similar things. Von Franz, according to Jane Ferguson, has analysed 65,000 dreams. She believes that dreams are normal, and if we are not connected with our dreaming life we may develop a neurosis. Attendance to our dreams is the healthiest thing we can do. They show us how to find meaning in our lives, how to fulfil our destiny, how to realise the greater potential of life within us.

Both my dreams and the Sudanese lady's dreams discussed in this chapter have referred to the prophetic elements of dreams within the realm of the African cultural context. Dreams come for a reason. Consequently, when a dream appears we think about it and examine it critically in search of a realistic interpretation.

Chapter 3

African Societal Beliefs

Africans, as described by John Mbiti (1969), are 'notoriously religious'.[1] Their deep-rooted spiritual beliefs have enabled them to live in harmony with Mother Earth. 'Religion is the strongest element in the traditional background, and exerts probably the greatest influence upon the thinking and living of the people concerned.'[2] Because of this strong belief in God their destiny, which is an expression of their existentialism, is linked with their actions. But why do Africans believe in messages which they receive through dreams? Historically, it has been believed that dreams have a purpose for mankind. Africans do believe in dreams because they believe their ancestors still influence the society and help and guide the living in their day-to-day activities. It is believed the dead, or the ancestors, are 'alive' somewhere and help the living in making decisions. For this reason the living always consult the oracle to see what the ancestors have to say. The reason why Africans believe in messages will be elaborated further in this chapter, in which I give examples of dreams from different people.

Some dreams are straightforward and some are complicated. Dreamers need independent help in interpreting their dreams. These experts in dream interpretation are expected to interpret correctly, without exaggeration. A distortion or incorrect interpretation of dreams causes repetition in dreams. And until a correct interpretation is offered, dream-recurring becomes a common feature in one's dream world.

In this chapter I will examine the significance of dreams in some African societies. Many African societies believe that dreams can guide them to their destiny and to a large extent help to shape their cultural relationships with each other. But, sad to say, very few of their dreams have been recorded. People have relied on oral tradition as a means of preserving culture. There is a prevalent view among many African societies that dreams occur at a particular time when the gods intend to reveal something which is unknown to human beings. Consequently, dreams convey warnings or messages pertaining to one's future. In this process, ancestral spirits act as intermediaries. People in Africa have been cured of serious illnesses by listening to dreams and implementing messages contained therein.

In order to demonstrate the essential ideas in dreams and how they work in the African context, it will be useful to examine the main features of African religion. African traditional religious (ATR) have characteristics which they share with many other religions, including Judaism, Christianity and Islam.

The idea of divinity in ATR

As in Islam and Judaeo-Christian cultures, ATR holds that God is a super-being who has command over all other creatures. There are writers on African society, e.g. Parrinder (1975), who have maintained that belief in a supreme God is due to the influence of a hierarchical society, and that God is nothing more than a glorified chief or ancestor.[3] In spite of this ancestor perception of God, it is a common belief in Africa that there is God who is above everything. It is believed that there is a Supreme Being who existed before everything else and this Supreme Being sends his warnings through ancestors. To support the idea of a Supreme God in Africa, Idowu (1973), in quoting Baudins, argues that, although deeply imbued with polytheism, Africans have not lost the idea of the true God.[4]

Peoples of Africa believe in one God although He is known by different names and descriptions. In East Africa God is called Lezer, a name also used in Zambia, the upper Congo and Tanzania. In Kenya the Kikuyu believes in a Supreme God called Murungu. In Malawi He is called by the same name but with an 'l' (Mulungu). In Nigeria the Ibos call Him Chineka, while the Yorubas call Him Oluwa. In Sudan, God is known by several names among the African tribes – the Nuer call Him Kuoth, the Dinke call Him Nhalic and the Shuluk call Him Juok. The Mende people of Sierra Leone believe in a creator called Mgwo.

It is believed that through God's commands everything happens. The Supreme Being could cause certain things to happen. My mother told me that in her childhood days people prayed to God (Mulungu) for rain whenever it failed and in times of drought and famine. They would gather at one place, normally on a hilltop in a form of a table-mountain, but sometimes in the chief's compound, to conduct these rituals. And since rain actually fell after such prayers people had strong faith in their rituals. And they believed God was behind this. To them God was all-merciful, the provider and fountain of all life. God was also believed to punish sinners, criminals, murderers, adulterers, etc. Thus, God was the all-powerful symbol of righteousness and justice and arbiter between human conflicts. All in all He wanted peace on earth. For this reason people are generally good to each other for fear that if you do harm to a fellow human being God takes revenge on behalf of your adversary. This may seem to be a contradiction in terms. But it was this vary flexibility which enabled Christianity to spread in Africa so rapidly.

The ATR can be summarised as follows:

i)   It is God the Supreme Being who has power to do all things.
ii)   The spirits of the forefathers are in direct contact with God.
iii) The forefathers spirits can plead with God for favours on behalf of their descendants.
iv)   Forefathers can be contacted through the oracles in the manner described above to ask them to plead with God to provide particular favours.

The role of intermediaries in ATR

In Judaeo-Christian culture people speak of prophets, saints and angels who serve as intermediaries between man and his/her God. In the New Testament this was slightly changed when Jesus taught that people would go to his father through him and him alone. In Islam prophet Muhammad is the mediating bridge between God and man. In ATR the equivalents of these intermediaries are the ancestral spirits and the oracle/priests. The oracle has the power of seeing things, while the priest's duty is to communicate with the oracles.

Ancestor and life after death

In ATR, like many other religions, people believe in life after death. Hetherwick, as quoted by Ranger *et al.* (1972), wrote the following about the soul or spirit in Malawi: 'At death a man's *lisoka* left the earth for all time and went to *Mulungu*, i.e. entered the spirit world. There it had powers which it never had on earth, but the living prayed only to *Mulungu* and never to *masoka*.'[5] The elaborate burial ceremonies which form part of the funeral rituals of many African communities are seen as making life in the hereafter more comfortable for the dead. Consequently it is also logically believed that the dead have a significant influence over the living. More importantly, if the deceased was a village headman, a grandfather, or a great-grandmother, they are given free will to choose their burial sites from where they can continue their task of guiding the living. Ranger *et al.* support this when they write: 'The ancestors are often thought of as the living dead. In many societies they participate in the life of the community.'[6]

For this reason people of the same tribe or clan would live near the graveyard in order to look after the dead. In prehistorical and historical times this belief was so strong that chiefs were buried together with living, beautiful girls who were said to be their maids. They would lie beside him in the grave to keep him company. The graveyards are well looked after and there are instances when the dead appear if the graveyard is neglected, prompting people to take swift action by way of repairs. The dead can appear again if action is not taken.

A friend by the name of Matilda Munthali was visited by her sister in January 1990. Matilda's sister is a teacher in Malawi. I went to see her in Birmingham. Her sister told me that their mother, who had died years before, appeared to her in a dream, asking her to erect a cement pillar at her grave. She ignored the dream. However, the dream, kept on being repeated. When she had the dream for the third time she decided to tell her family and they did as advised in the dream. Once this cement pillar was built at the graveyard the dream stopped too.

As stated earlier, the dream is repeated if the interpretation is distorted. I was in Malawi in August 1990. A lady called Mai Nambewe, aged sixty, told me a story. She used to have a recurring dream. In her dream she could see her father, who had died, just glaring at her without saying anything. Different diviners tried to give their interpretation but the lady still continued having the dream.

Later on, someone who knew her family very well interpreted it. All that the family needed to do was to clear the graveyard. The cement pillar was overgrown by grass and it was difficult to tell there was a graveyard at all. Once the graveyard had been cleared, the lady stopped dreaming. The woman who interpreted the dream apparently had it in her mind that the family had neglected the graveyard because graves ought to be treated with great respect. This point is echoed by Ranger, who writes: 'Ancestral graves of both Sultans and chiefs (or chiefs and headmen, in Mitchell's terminology), were regarded with the same veneration in Tundura during the 1940s as was observed at the beginning of the century by Hetherwick in southern Malawi. To take what is the head-stone of a chief's grave would be an offence punishable by death.[7] Ranger also adds what Lamburn records: 'The late Sultan Mtalika is known to have killed a boy of whom he was extremely fond just because the boy had the audacity to take a roll of cloth off the grave of the deceased uncle of Mtalika.'[8]

All this originates from fear. It is as if Sultan Mtalika was saying to himself, 'The spirits will do harm to us if I don't take any action against what the boy has done.' Fear here symbolises the fact that people believe the dead watch over what we do and communicate with us.

Hence, it is also believed that when people die they can come and be reborn in the same family. For this reason you find people's names repeating within the same family. A glamorous story which took place in a Nigerian village could be narrated here. A grandfather had six fingers and it so happened that one of his grandchildren was childless. The grandfather told her not to worry because she was going to have him as her son when he died. Upon the grandfather's death the granddaughter conceived and gave birth to a baby boy with six fingers . . .

A similar story was narrated to me by a Zambian student, Charles Sakanya, at Liverpool University. He said that if a child is born and is given a name which does not belong to it, it cries heavily without stopping. If people don't know the name of the ancestoral relations to give to the child, they may be inclined to think he is sick and take him to hospital. Unfortunately the child doesn't stop crying. Eventually a member of the family or any other person in the village may dream a name. In the morning they share their dream experience with members of the family. Upon bearing the dream, the family consult a diviner and the diviner interprets it, saying they need to give the name of that deceased person who appeared in the dream. Immediately after the child is given that name he stops crying. This has contributed to the belief that people are reborn, as we shall see in Chapter 4. In this sense it means that the person who appeared in the dream is this child who is reborn.

There are also ancestors who are unknown to the dreamer. It could be that my grandfather, who died before I was born, appears to me in a dream telling me of something. In the morning I relate the story to my mother and describe how the ancestor looked in my dream. The elderly will then take the dream seriously, saying there must be a reason for my grandfather to appear to me.

It is more important that I have never seen him. Different diviners would be consulted until one of them mentions the thing which would convince those elders. If that thing has been mentioned and is agreed unanimously, then it is what the grandfather required or asked for. The interpretation is then taken seriously and the things that the diviner has mentioned would be taken into account. In this way the diviner has convinced a lot of elderly people. The village or the family does exactly what the diviner requires. If it's killing a goat or a cow for sacrifice it will be done without hesitation. Even if people had no goats of their own they would travel long distances to buy one.

Dreaming of the unknown deceased is also supported by M. G. Whisson et al., in their book, Religious and Social Change in Southern Africa. They write: 'Among the ancestors who appear in dreams some are known and some are unknown. Those who are unknown are those who died long ago before the person was born. Those who are recognised in dreams are those who died during the lifetime of the living.'[9]

Joackim Pikiti from Zambia also told me that if a woman is pregnant, and either the wife or husband has a recurring dream of a person who died during that period of pregnancy they would share the dream and would know that the gods want to give the baby the name of the deceased who appeared in the dream.

Communication with ancestors through dreams plays a critical role in African culture. Dreams provide a medium through which the living may come in contact with the invisible or spirits as we shall see later. The latter, however, may appear to give approval to proposals, to show displeasure about what is happening or even to reveal secrets or help in cases of sickness. All these show how useful a dream is in African society.

Joackim told me a further story which happened in Zambia in 1987. An uncle to Joackim died. He was a very respectable man. He had much land before he died, and he employed a girl to work in it, and to do other jobs in the farm. His death was sudden and he had not paid off the girl her money before he died. After one week the dead man appeared to Joackim's aunt, saying, 'Tell my son to give something to the girl'. This dream was repeated three times, the deceased still saying, 'I am troubled, tell my son to pay the girl.' Later on the aunt decided to go and see this girl in her village. She paid off the money and told them about the dream, to discover that the girl was having dreams about the same thing. The man who died was telling her to go and collect the money. She too had this dream three times. The girl was afraid to share the dream with her mother. There was a time when it was an insult in some parts of Africa to mention the name of a deceased person. Apparently, that was the reason why the girl never mentioned it to anyone.

She only mentioned it this time when Joackim's aunt visited her family. If she had never shared her dream experience, the girl would have kept her own dream to herself. But she was encouraged by hearing the aunt talking about it. However, once the money was paid off the aunt never dreamt again, and nor did the girl. Joackim told me that it's always his aunt who dreams in their family and whatever she dreams has to be acted upon; if not, the dream keeps on recurring. This shows that there are special people to whom the gods send their message.

Joackim Pikiti and Charles Sakanya, studying at Liverpool University, told me yet another interesting story involving twin brothers. One of the twins died. The twin who was left kept having a recurring dream, but never shared it with anyone. The boy who died was calling his brother each night to come and join him. The living boy tried to forget, but the dream persisted. The boy wrote a long letter explaining all that was happening and that he felt he should go and join his brother. He left the letter in his room and went on the flyover and killed himself.

A girl from Malawi by the name of Ayende (Gowa) had a sister who died, leaving some children. After three years the sister appeared to her in a dream. She sat down and was actually talking to her and also looked to her with a sad face. She told her she had neglected her children. Some of the deceased sister's children were staying with her. It was financially a burden to her. She told the children to go to her village, since living in town was very costly. She wanted the children to stay with her mother. But with this intervening dream she changed her plans and kept the children with her.

Although she did not personally consult the oracle, the expectation here is that if she had she would have been told the sister was offended by the way her children had been treated and among other things might prescribe that a white hen be offered in sacrifice to appease the sister. In most cases the interpretation given by mediums indicates the will of the ancestors. This story, then, is an example of the spirits of a dead relation appearing to show displeasure about what is happening.

As stated above, one could say that the dead or the deceased participated in decision-making. Ayende was on the verge of sending her deceased sister's children home. But the deceased sister appeared, saying, 'You are neglecting my children'. Without the dream the children would have definitely gone to stay in a village, so perhaps the mother did not want her children to stay with anyone else apart from Ayende. Ranger et al. also support the idea of the dead participating in decision-making. Thus they write, 'The dead kings, through their Linomboti* also have an important role in the policy-making of the country. The dead spirits are also consulted for guidance based on decisions taken under comparable circumstances earlier in Lozi history.'[10]

* Linomboti: intermediaries

Ancestor worship and sacrifices

Ancestor worship is not only an African phenomenon. It is also practised in many other parts of the world. David Stent, in his book *Religious Studies Made Simple*, writes: 'Certainly evidence of the practice throughout the history of mankind can be found in many parts of the world, notable Africa, China and in Easter Island.[11] He explains: There are a number of reasons why people in various parts of the world have worshipped their ancestors. Some have been motivated by respect for the dead and the hope that they might be in a position to help the living. Others have been persuaded to worship them out of fear, terrified of what an irate soul might be tempted to do if not propitiated by sufficient sacrifices or offering.'[12] Rowie (1960) also writes on the same issue in his book *Primitive Religion*, that 'in Africa the ancestor-worship appearing in Siberia and carried to extremes in the higher Chinese civilisation is a widespread phenomenon – certainly for more so than "fetishism".'[13] What Rowie writes is true. But ancestor worship is normally associated with respect for the dead, as Stent puts it.

Some, when they are worshipping the ancestors, take it to mean they are worshipping God. This is because it is believed the dead go to unite with the gods or God. It is also believed the ancestors have survived death and that they are living in a world of their own, the spiritual world. Ancestors are regarded as part of people's families. I attended a conference in 1976 in Nairobi where professor John Mbiti, the famous writer on ATR, came to deliver a talk. In his presentation he argued that ancestors or the dead do not go away completely. 'They hang around in trees.'

A friend of mine, Lydia Adebora, who is at the moment working with Liverpool Housing Trust as an administrator provides useful insight into the issue of ancestral worshipping. She writes: 'Worshipping the gods or deities is done in Yoruba land and most tribes in Nigeria. Worshipping of the gods is done because it is a way and means of communicating with our God and our ancestors, of having our prayers answered, as well as of being protected from all forms of ills and disasters. It can be a way of forming a stronger bond in the already extended family systems, providing support morally and advice to the younger ones. In Yoruba land, there exist different types of gods or deities and each one rep-

resents a symbol of what we come into contact with in our everyday life and which we believe must not be ignored.'

Since the dead are respected and worshipped, it is believed
they do have an influence on us. For this reason it is an African
phenomenon or tradition to consult the oracle and see whether or
not the ancestors are in support of an action a person proposes to
take before he actually does it. The belief is that anything which
does not receive the support of the ancestor is bound to fail.

There is a very interesting event that took place in Malawi. A
couple remained childless for a long time. The story was that,
before the marriage, the man had consulted the oracle to see
whether it was right to marry this girl whom he admired. The
oracle told him his dead father was not a supporter of the marriage. The man did not listen to what the oracle said. He went
ahead with the marriage, but ended up having no children. He
went again to consult the oracle, and the oracle said that it was
because the dead father was still not happy with the marriage.
Unfortunately, the man decided to divorce his wife. He married
another lady, who received the ancestral support as revealed
through the oracle, and the marriage was blessed with many
children. His first wife also got married to another man and had
children by him.

The idea of ancestor worship is nothing but worshipping God
himself. The dead serve only as intermediaries. Sometimes misfortune comes to a person because he believes it to be that way.
Normally ancestor worship is associated with sacrifice. You cannot
really put a demarcation between the two. Each time one mentions
ancestor worship the sacrifice is there because the ancestors always
demand sacrifices. For this reason I have treated ancestor worship
and sacrifice as relating to each other.

I could probably relate the story of my own brother, Oliver
Chinkwita. He worked in Zimbabwe for many years. Later on he
came home and found my father had died. People in the village
advised him to authorise some women to brew beer and slaughter
a cow or a goat and make some offerings in respect of his father,
which would have meant calling everyone in the village to come
and eat at our house: a sort of a feast. My brother ignored everything. Since then he has been very unfortunate in many ways.

A burned mother

Joackim and Charles, referred to earlier, told me the story of a mother who got burned. The mother had a daughter who had two children. The daughter suffered from some mental problems. She attacked and cut her mother while asleep. She then attacked her two children. Fortunately someone heard and saved the children. The daughter set the house on fire before she ran away. The mother was burned to death.

It is believed that death like that brings misfortune to the whole family. The rest of the family can die if nothing is done. As it was, one member of the family had a dream in which she was told to go and take some herbals. She shared the dream with the rest of the family, they knew what it was and went to take the herbals. They put the herbs in a clay pot and poured some warm water for the whole family to bathe in. While bathing, people are required to swear, such as, 'You devil, I don't know you. Keep away from us.'

If anyone died in that way – being burned – they had to be buried in a special way, otherwise the spirits would get angry and kill every member of the family. There is a general consensus on this in Zambia and Lesotho, as confirmed in the following interview I had with a Lesotho lady.

An interview with Nchafatso Mothea

Nchafatso was studying at Liverpool University for an MA degree when this interview was recorded. She said her people believed in the gods but it depended largely on the individual. 'What are you referring to when you say "the gods"? Do you mean our Living God?' I asked. "No," she replied, 'I mean our ancestors. People who died years ago. If, for instance, a person dies people are supposed to slaughter a cow, so that the hide can be used as a blanket to wrap him in burial. If this is not done, for economic reasons, a deceased person appears to one member of the family, saying, "You did not provide me with a skin." What the family does now is to make sure they slaughter one and make the skin a bit soft. The family uses it as a mat so long as this is done for that purpose. If this is done the family cannot have that kind of dream again.

'The same is true in cases involving incurable diseases. The sick person's family is authorised to slaughter a cow or a goat and leave it uncooked overnight. In the morning the family cooks it and eats it with everyone in the village. It is believed that the family gets cured in that way. By leaving the meat uncooked overnight they interpret it to mean the gods have eaten first. Of course during this night other traditional rituals are performed to help the sick man get well.'

Nchafatso later indicated that this works psychologically. The same rituals might not work for others. She further told me that her grandmother was a diviner. She acquired medical knowledge not from school but through spiritual possession, which saw her performing a number of incredible healings. She could dream about how she should go about her practice and how to solve problems. Supposing someone was sick in a village or a member of her family became sick, she could be told in her dream to go and take particular herbals. She was famous to the extent that dreams were not just dreams to her. They meant a lot. They directed her. Unfortunately, the grandmother died in 1975.

Lydia Adebola (Nigeria)

Lydia also wrote on dream, as follows. Priests and priestesses also play an important role in interpreting people's dreams. For example, if anyone has a dream which they find disturbing or of which they would like to know the meaning, they go to the priests or priestesses who, after consulting the oracle, will tell them the meaning of the dream; and if it calls for a situation where something evil or bad is going to happen to the dreamer or his relative or friend, the priest will suggest the next course of action to take to appease the gods.

What the priest does is to take a curved dish – wood or clay. He puts in this dish white beads or white sea sand. He can sometimes use kola-nuts. He throws it on the floor. If it faces upwards that is a sign of good omen. If all face down, it is bad luck. In this case they take it to mean the god are not happy and try to find out why, and what they must do. They then offer sacrifice to appease the gods. Dreams such as falling down are a bad omen in most cases, and those about flying mean good omen or success in its simplest form. Equally there are some dreams which do not need any interpretation, more importantly in the case of healing dreams, where the gods reveal to people where they can get medicine if someone is sick.

George Simpson supports what Lydia writes. He asserts, 'Among the Yoruba, dreams are believed to portray future events and distant happenings. A juice or a powder may be placed on or near the eyes to stimulate the power of occult sight. Diviners determine which dreams are symbolical or go by opposites require interpretation.'[14]

From what I gathered during the course of this interview, most dreams in Africa are associated with the wrath of God. Anything unusual, people would say, God is angry with us. Stent, in his book *Religious Studies Made Simple'*, mentions the same thing. 'Wrath of God, therefore, had to be appeased.' There are also instances where it need not to be a dream, but just a mystic happening.

Margaret Mbonya (Tanzania)

Margaret was studying for her B. Ed degree in Home Economics at Calder College (Liverpool University). She told me that in a certain Tanzanian village a man went to his field. When going home he went to wash in a river. There he found a big fish. The fish talked and said: 'Take me to the chief,' The man was shocked but he could not do anything except carry the fish to the chief. There the village gathered to see the wonders of a fish speaking. The fish said, 'Chief, and people of the village, your ancestors are very angry, since you don't take care of this village.' The chief and village sacrificed and cleared the area and made sure it was clean.

Hunting dreams

Charles from Zambia, referred to earlier, reported that 'just supposing you are going hunting tomorrow and you dream of a man who died some time ago and was a good hunter himself – that means good luck, you are going to kill many animals, even seven.

But when you come home you have to sacrifice part of your haul to appease the gods for blessing you. You are to kill the animal and take the blood and pour it on the rubber tree. The rubber tree is normally planted outside the house for that purpose. Pouring the blood in a hole is an indication of giving to the gods. Supposing the hunter does not offer sacrifice and he goes hunting again and brings back nothing. People in his village, or his fellow hunters, would say he thought he was clever by not thanking the gods for blessing him with the animals. Now he will never kill one at all for the rest of his hunting.'

Hunting dreams are useful to hunters not only in Zambia but in much of Africa, because they encourage them before they actually go to the forest. Revd. Canon Callaway, writing about the Amazulu of South Africa, quotes the dream of one hunter: 'I saw some buffaloes during the night, we were hunting them; they were just like cattle.'[15]

This dreamer shared his dream experience with some hunters. The shared dream encouraged them. When they went things were as the man saw them in his dream: 'When we found the buffalo they were just like cattle, as he told us; we killed them, and did not get so much as a scratch.'[16]

Medicine dreams

There are also instances when people dream about medicine. It happens sometimes that a child is sick for quite a long time. The family tries different therapeutic preparations, but all in vain. All of a sudden a grandmother dreams that she has to go to such and such a herbalist and the child will be cured. The family does as advised in the dream and the child is indeed cured.

Equally, a lady can be sick for ages and everything fails. In the dream she is told to take some roots and with those roots she is cured. This largely depends on her faith. You can't get cured if you don't believe.

What is stated above could be supported by a story told to Taylor (1969), who did research in Zimbabwe. A man called Benedict was sick in hospital for quite a long time. He was suffering from eye trouble and could not see properly, and his doctor told him he needed an operation. He agreed, but that night his father appeared to him in a dream. He looked tall and had a long beard, and was white, but he knew it was his father. He gave him a long white robe with red cuffs and a red girdle. He said to him, 'There is no cure for you in this place, but traditional herbalists will cure you.'[17]

The next morning the doctor came and wanted to give him an anaesthetic in readiness for the operation. He refused and requested a discharge, which the doctor reluctantly granted two weeks later. The sick man tried the herbal medicines but he did not feel any better. He dreamt again. His father said, 'My son Benedict, wake up. Go outside and cut down the tree standing by the road, burn it and look at it as it burns, burn it also with a castor-oil beam.'[18] He did as instructed and was healed; he could use his eyes as before.

Witchcraft dreams

Angela Kafumba, whose husband is studying for his PhD in Economics with Liverpool University, and is a qualified nurse herself, shared with me her aunt's dream. Her aunt, Mrs Anne Gondwe, aged forty-seven, dreamt that somebody had placed medicine in her garden. The idea was that if her son passed there he would fall down. She shared her dream experiences with her husband. Early in the morning they decided to go and call on a ng'anga diviner. The story turned out to be true. There was a big snake in the garden and the snake would have killed the boy, who used to play in the garden.

The ng'anga revealed that this was the devilish work of their own home attendant and he admitted having plotted to kill the boy on advise from another man. The family sacked the attendant. The son was given herbal medicine and discharged the snake through the anal passage. It looked exactly the same snake which was in the garden where the medicine was. The boy would have died but he is now alive. Angela saw this with her own eyes.

How witchcraft works in Africa is difficult to tell since it is a secret. Idowu, in his book *African Traditional Religion*, argues: 'The question of how witches operate must be connected with the problem of evil in general. Until we can unravel the problem of evil, the question of the methods and techniques of witchcraft will remain a perplexity to a great extent.'[19] However, my interest in the above dream is how the dream helped save the life of this boy, who would otherwise have died. Dream has helped shape African society.

General dreams

There are also instances where you can dream that such-and-such a person hates you. Sometimes it's a person whom you really respected and did not think could do harm to you. That dream has to be taken into account, not ignored, since it is believed that dream does not lie. A Nigerian girl now living in Liverpool had this kind of dream. She dreamt she had quarrelled with her best friend, who she had known for a long time, and wondered as to what sort of dream it was. She found that dream very disagreeable.

Eventually the girl was admitted to hospital. Her friend brought her favourite food each time she visited her in hospital. This time her friend came without bringing anything. She knew what it was because of the dream. She also confesses that she would not have eaten even if she was to bring the food for her. Apparently the other girl just forced herself to come to the hospital. They had a big quarrel after the girl had been discharged. The other girl was reporting unnecessary things to the first girl's husband. This created a big fight. In such cases, the dream helps you to know your enemies and you treat them with caution. Revd. Canon Callaway (referred to earlier) supports this. He writes: 'If during sleep you dream of a man whom you do not thoroughly know to be of such a character that he may do you an injury; yet if in your sleep you dream that he suddenly stabs you, not openly, but by stealth, when you awake you are much amazed and say, "Oh, forsooth I thought such one a really good man. And does he hate me: I do not know in what respect I have injured him." And you continue on your guard against the man, believing that the dream does not tell a lie.'[20]

Such dreams help one to be on guard. You try by all means to avoid that person. Sometimes it happens that the person you dreamt of doing harm to you will come to confess that he intended to do evil but does not now want to. He would tell you everything he had in mind.

George Cole of Sierra Leone

George is now working as a Senior Health Promotion Officer. He shared with me the dream his grandmother had while he was young. His grandmother told him not to go to school that morning, saying that she had a bad dream the previous night. But George did not listen. He went to school. He had a quarrel with one of his classmates. They ended up fighting to such an extent that George was suspended from school. They wanted to expel him completely, but fortunately his uncle was a headmaster. So he pleaded that they should only suspend him. As it was George stayed off for one full term.

He shared with me another dream. His father died when he himself was one year old. His mother then decided to marry again. George's grandmother prevented her from doing so. She had had a bad dream. She dreamt that the man her daughter wanted to marry was very cruel and was beating her very badly. George's mother did not listen. She proceeded with her arrangements. The grandmother left her to do as she wanted. She got married to this man. George told me in his own words, 'What a pity, for my mother has suffered terribly since she got married'.

Mai Natsothe

While in Malawi in August 1990, I talked to a lady in our village who is now in her seventies. Her name is Mai Natsothe. She is one of my father's relations. She told me she had had a dream a while before. The dream told her our village was going to expand. The dream came like a puzzle to her. She did not know its meaning. Her mother was a diviner and she had also learned dream interpretation. But this she could not interpret. She tried to think: perhaps people in our village would multiply by having lots and lots of children. But she could still not see this happening, since there are only few houses in our village. However, she left the dream as it was.

The fact of the matter is that with the recent influx of Mozambique war-displaced persons, the village is expanding at an alarmingly rapid rate. There is no available land to cultivate. The whole land is taken up by refugee camps.

Dream interpretation

Sandra St Rose, who is at the moment working with Liverpool Social Services as a Senior Social Worker, dreams a lot. She is from the West Indies. Her mother is gifted in dream interpretation. Thus she shares with her mother each dream she has. She had a dream one night in which one of her colleagues was asking her to give him ten pence. Sandra refused, remarking, 'Am I a money lender?' The following morning she met this very same boy; the boy, upon seeing Sandra, asked if she would lend him ten pence. Sandra said in a joking way, 'Am I a money lender?' She still gave him the 10p that he wanted. She then remembered the dream.

In another dream Sandra dreamt of her friend Liz, who is also a social worker with Liverpool Social Services. Sandra had not seen Liz for quite a long time, because Liz had gone on a course. However, in a dream Sandra dreamt of Liz and that she had quarrelled with her boyfriend. The following morning Sandra was out driving when she saw Liz, and Sandra remembered the dream. She told Liz about it. Sandra said, 'I was dreaming about you and your boyfriend last night.' Liz told her they were no longer together as they had quarrelled.

General dreams

1. Sandra dreamt of lots and lots of green vegetables, okra and green fruits. She told her mother, and her mother said lots of green means money. The same week Sandra got a letter from the Inland Revenue that she had paid too much income tax, and they refunded her £600.
2. To dream of soft fruits means a birth in the family or a friend's family.
3. To dream of being attacked by rats means you are surrounded by enemies. Someone is trying to get you.
4. To dream of lots of meat and lots of houses means death in your family or a family which you know very well. Sandra had this dream early in January 1991. She shared it with her mother and the mother said, 'Death'. There was a funeral the same week in the family of one of

their relative's. The dreams above were interpreted by
Sandra's mother.

5.   Falling-out of teeth means losing a relative in the family
     shortly after the dream. It has got other interpretations,
     but this is the most popular.
6.   Flying denotes success, in most cases, or passing exams,
     but some interpret it differently as meaning long life.
7.   A big tree: to dream of a big tree with green leaves, and
     you see its come out and the tree falls down with a big
     noise, symbolises a death in the family.
8.   A large river or lake also signifies death.
9.   To dream of drinking beer means one will drink poison.
10. Dreaming of someone sick means long life.
11. Climbing a tree means promotion at work.
12. Fire signifies misfortune.
13. A recurring dream means taking action.
14. If a girl is expecting a baby and she dreams of fish or
     water it is thought to mean a baby girl. If she dreams of
     a snake, that means a baby boy.
15. Catching fish means receiving money from somewhere
     unexpectedly.
16. A wedding indicates a funeral; also loss of money.

The interpretations above are what I have gathered during the
course of my research. Most of them are from Zimbabwe, Malawi,
Zambia, Lesotho, West Indies and Nigeria.

Christian ministry dreams

Dream has also played a great role in Christian ministry. Most
theological students who were with me told me that it was because
of dreams that they came to theological college. Some had very
big jobs in government but had left because it was revealed in a
dream that they would serve the ministry of God. Most church
ministers witnessed Jesus Christ calling them in a dream. Bengt
Sundkler (1963) also supports this in his book *Christian Ministry in
Africa*. He writes on the close relationship of dream and vocation.
An evangelist in the Lake Victoria area states, 'Things happen,
and things that happen have first been dreamt in a dream; then

they happen.'[21] Sundkler was here referring to the dreams which made him join the catechism class. A Congo pastor makes a useful distinction: 'There are two kinds of dream: firstly, dreams about things and conditions of which the dreamer has prior knowledge; secondly, exceptional dreams about things and conditions of which he has no such knowledge. The latter are inspired by God. If vocation is channelled through a dream of the second kind, it should be taken seriously in the Synod.'[22]

How this pastor puts it is how I understand dreams in Africa. People believe some dreams come from God and those have to be listened to and acted upon. To dream about being a church minister is to dream about going to theological college. Some people have given away all their possessions. They become satisfied with the little money they receive. It is believed God blesses the money, and it multiplies. Revd. Magombo of Malawi Presbyterian church was a policeman earning quite a good salary, but abandoned that job and joined the ministry because of a dream, believing that God blesses the money which the ministers receive at the church.

A Methodist, Kimbundu Angola Carpenter, who earned an income three times higher even than that of the pastor, gave up his business in order to join the ministry. These men, as Sundkler puts it, represent a very important section of the ministry in Africa today. They and their many colleagues throughout Africa have, in spite of very great hardship, found an assurance which a Zulu pastor expressed as: 'The little money which pastors earn is blessed money.'[23]

I have shown in this chapter how the dream has helped in shaping African society. Dreams have helped people in Africa to live in harmony with each other, and to reconcile their grievances. Dreams have helped people to know where to go and take the right herbals to heal their sickness. The ancestors have continuously guided and influenced African society in everyday life. The ancestors are believed to have survived death and are still living in another world and come and communicate with us.

Chapter 4

Reincarnation Experiences in Dreams
BARBARA LEE AND OTHER CASE STUDIES

That people die is a fact of creation and natural existence. It is suggested by some that people after death are reborn into a new human being and by implication that the people we see today are in fact the same people that existed centuries before. This seems to be a mixture of myth and 'fact' and beyond logic and science. But could they possibly be divine? There is, the suggestion continues, a growing number of people who strongly believe in reincarnation as a consolation when they are about to die. This has come to be known as Near-Death Experience. It is a consolation because they tend to argue that after all death is not the end of everything: there will be a rebirth process thereafter.

Thus, some go to a fortune-teller in the hope that they will be told about their past life and the life in front of them. I was once asked by friends to accompany them on one of these visits. They were disappointed when I turned the invitation down and argued that only God holds the future, for He alone knows about us. Discussions of fortune-telling and transmigration constitute an ongoing debate at Parkside Hostel. Dreaming along these lines is also a fascinating subject and some people have had reincarnation dreams, which are the discussion topic of this chapter.

One of my colleagues at work once asked, in a discussion group, whether it was true that people turn into an animal when they come back to life after death: that is, when they have been reincarnated. Another responded, 'Not really coming back as an animal.

One comes back in the human form only that you are at this time being born in a different family albeit of the same clan. In other words, you are born of the same grandparents.' But can one really remember about the past? 'Yes.'

One of the girls narrated a story of two children who could remember where they lived before. People went and actually saw the place and proved it to be true. The girl said this had been shown on BBC2. She continued arguing that even in biblical terms the soul is separated from the body at the time of death. Where does this soul go? Logically the person being born by the second mother is actually a person reborn from an existing soul.

Barbara stated that she personally finds it very strange that the Bible does not believe in reincarnation. She added that one day she was thinking seriously about this subject and thought of the early Christians. 'Did they not ask Jesus whether he was Elijah?' Yes, they did. Barbara asked what did that mean, because she does not know much about the Bible. To her mind she thinks the people who asked this question were thinking about reincarnation.

I told Barbara that she might be right and I had a discussion with my line manager Phil Purvis (Liverpool Social Services). He told me that he believes in reincarnation. He was surprised when I indicated that I did not believe in transformation. He said that he strongly believes in it and has actually met people who are able to remember about their past life. I was, to some extent, fascinated, although I do not really believe in reincarnation. Some, however, do remember what they used to do subconsciously and try to think of doing it again. How far this is true is another matter.

Transmigration seems to me to be wishful thinking. It seems to be something which is a way of comforting oneself, a phenomenon of old age. Interestingly it had been in my mind that if I was to be reincarnated I would have wished to live a very exemplary life, a life which would have pleased my Lord. I have always been dissatisfied with my way of living. But since reincarnation seems to be impossible, in my view, the only logical thing to do is to change one's conduct and live a righteous life while one is still alive.

Those who believe in reincarnation have, however, referred to Christ's words: 'Unless one is born anew, he cannot see the Kingdom of God.'[1] But this has nothing to do with reincarnation. Jesus meant to be born again as a creation new in Him or in Christ.

Paul the Apostle also talked about the new creation. 'Therefore, if any one is in Christ, he is a new creation; the old has passed away, behold, the new has come.' (2 Cor. 5, v. 17, RSV). It is therefore easy to mix this new creation with reincarnation. In fact, what Paul talked about is not even after death but the very moment one gives oneself to Christ one becomes a new person. Therefore, if anyone is in Christ he is a new creation; the old has passed away, behold the new has come. (2 Cor. 5. 17).

The rhetorical question contained in Paul's letter to the Romans provides some insight into the relationship between baptism and being born again in Christ. Paul wrote, 'Do you know that all of us who have been baptised into Jesus were baptised into death, so that as Christ was raised from the death by the glory of the father we too might walk in newness of life.'[2]

Paul taught that if we have been united with Christ in a death like his, we shall certainly be united with him in a resurrection like his. He talks of our old self being crucified with Jesus so that the sinful body might be destroyed, and might no longer be enslaved to sin. Thus, if we have died with Christ we believe that we shall also live with him.[3]

The sinking disappearance, and emergence of the believer from the baptismal wave, belong to baptism in its full dramatic form, image identification with death, burial and resurrection of the Lord. The sacrament unfolds the implications of faith, and interprets it. Faith means more than reliance on Christ, on God who raised him from the dead; it is the planting of man in Christ. For man dies Christ's death and rises into Christ's life. Burial of the human corpse represents a rupture with old terrestrial world.

Peak's commentary to the Romans states: 'If we can become coalescent (of one growth) with Christ by the likeness of his death; and by the faith baptism experience which copies Christ's death – we shall be equally so in respect of his resurrection as we come to know that our old nature was crucified with him'.[4]

It should be emphasised here that in his letter to the Romans Paul's reference to rebirth was in the context of resurrection in Christ, not reincarnation. So when Jesus talked about being reborn he meant spiritual change of life.

Reincarnation defined

Collins English Dictionary defines the word 'reincarnation' as the belief that on the death of the body the soul transmigrates to, or is born again in, anotherbody.[5] *Collier's Encyclopaedia* asserts that the new body in which the soul is said to be reincarnated may be human, animal, plant or inanimate.[6]

The soul

The *New Encyclopaedia Britannica (Micropaedia)* makes a distinction between body and soul. In theology the soul is defined as that part of the individual which partakes of divinity and is often considered to survive the death of the body.[7] Most Christians believe that the soul was created by God and take the soul to be separate from the body. God takes the soul or rather the soul goes to live with God immediately after the person had died.

The Greek idea of the soul varied among the great philosophers. Pythagoras maintained that the soul was of divine origin and existed before and after death. Plato and Socrates also accepted the immortality of the soul.[8] According to Plato the human soul is a complete bodiless entity in its own right. He believed in the soul as a separate entity from the body. He maintained that the soul "existed eternally before birth and will exist externally after death".[9] Aristotle did not teach personal immortality of the soul. His conception of the soul was obscure, though he did state that it was a form inseparable from the body.[10] He refuted Plato's theory by maintaining that a living human being is not two things but one. The Christians who followed Aristotle's teaching believed that life after death depended upon God.

However, the belief that the soul passes on to someone and starts a new life altogether seems to be a universal one, although some people have traditionally believed that only Hinduism and Buddhism, African Traditional Religion and that of the Aborigines in Australia believe in reincarnation. The Welsh have claimed that 'the doctrine of reincarnation began with the Celts far back in prehistory and that it was from them that it found its way to the East to flower in Hinduism and Buddhism'.[11] While those in the Pacific Islands, Indonesia, Micronesia and Melanesia believe in the transformation of human soul into an animal.

Herodotus, a Greek historian writing in the fifth century BC, said about the Egyptian beliefs, 'The soul at the death enters into some other living thing, comes to birth and after living through all creatures of land, sea and air in a cycle lasting three thousand years, it enters a human body once more at birth.'[12] The Egyptians also held that the entering of the human soul into a lower animal might be a punishment for sin.[13]

In Malawi, particularly among the Chewa, people believe that the dead do not go away completely. Their spirits or soul hang around in trees and they continue guiding mankind whenever they are in the wrong, or do not conform with traditions and societal culture. Whenever one goes astray the ancestral spirits appear to one in a dream in either guidance or rebuke. This is where you see the picture of that person which is an indication that she/he is living somewhere. Equally, Malawians believe that if a person has been a sinner he turns into an animal after death. That animal appears in the village where the funeral took place. In order to appease the spirits, elders call upon spirit specialists to give sacrifice and ask that the animal be retrieved to the death.

Usually, when these animals appear, people know that they're not ordinary animals. They are reflections of the dead or creations of the spiritual world. For instance, there used to come a very big python snake outside our house. My mother sought the help in a spirit appraiser, who performed a short ritual. The snake disappeared, and it never came back again. The man said it was a relation of my father, who had died earlier in our village.

An examination of psychological interpretation of reincarnation is in order at this stage. Carl Jung was compelled to invoke the ideas of pre-existence and rebirth. He stated in 'Memories, Dreams, Reflections:'

My life as I lived, had often seemed to me, like a story that has no beginning and no end, I had the feeling that I was a historical fragment, an excerpt for which the proceeding and succeeding text was missing. I could well imagine that I might have lived in former centuries and there encountered questions I was not yet able to answer, that I had to be born again because I had not fulfilled the task that was given to me. When I die, my deeds will follow along with me what I have done. In the meantime it was important that I do not stand empty hands,[14]

There are a lot of people who, like Jung, believe they have lived a good life, and are going to be reborn. To finish unfinished business, some take it as a reward. Jung, however, continues:

> In my case it must have been primarily a passionate urge towards understanding which brought about my birth, for that is the strongest element in my nature. This insatiable drive towards understanding has, as it were, created a consciousness in order to know what is and what happens, and in order to piece together mythic conceptions from the slender hints of the unknowable. He further states it might happen that I would not be reborn again so long as the world needed no such answer, and that it would be entitled to several hundred years peace until someone was once more needed who took an interest in these matters and could profitably tackle the task a new. I imagine that for a while a period of rest could ensure, until the stint I had done in my lifetime needed to be taken up again.[15]

Barbara Lee

Some people are inclined to think they existed before because of the strange dreams they experience. Here is a recorded dream of a young lady in her own words.

> My name is Barbara – I work in the caring profession. When I had this dream I was in my early twenties. About every three or four months I had the same dream. I live in a suburb of Liverpool called Speke. It is very close to Hale village. Hale is very old and comes under Cheshire. As an Anglo-Saxon settlement, very little is known about Hale but from 1066 onwards it is possible to trace the history of Hale, mostly from ancient court books and parchments and documents of various kinds.
>   In my dream it is nearly always dusk: not dark and not light. I am always alone, always I am searching for a road that does not exist. I see Hale village as it is today, but I am

searching for another turn-off that is not there. Sometimes I find myself arriving by car, or by bus or train, as though I am trying different ways of getting there so I might come across the road. at this time I am married with two little daughters. I am living in a house in Speke which overlooks the fields surrounding Hale. Often I would walk on a summer day with the children. It is a lovely village. I had the dream off and on maybe over a period of twelve months or so.

One night I had the dream again. There is in Hale what the local children call the 'conker park'. It is two large fields with a path leading through the middle. There are many large chestnut trees around the fields, hence the name 'conker park'. There is a small lodge at the entrance. I don't know if anyone lives there. This night I dream I was searching for the road around this small park. The following day I went into work and I happened to mention the dream to my friend, Pat.

Pat lives in Hale, I suppose that's why I told her. Pat said there is a road no one uses any more and it is through the park. At the back of the park there is a wood which has grown over what is left of the road. Pat had a book which she let me borrow, called 'The History of Hale.' It seems that through the woods the road continues, although one wouldn't know it now. At the end of this road stood a house called Hale Hall. It is in ruins now. It was very large, an early Jacobean house constructed by Gilbert Ireland. It was altered in 1674 by Gilbert's grandson, whose name was also Gilbert. The north front of the house was originally gabled from which bay windows projected below, but when the grandson Gilbert altered it, he arched over the recesses between the bay windows and built a brick wall to hide the gables. The wall has stone medallions and other ornaments.

The house was then complete and Sir Gilbert placed on the tower a stone with these words inscribed on it: 'Built by Sir Gilbert Ireland KT and Dame Margaret. AODI, 1674'. Now the house is in ruins and the stone tablet has been removed to the house of the American Ireland family in Cleveland, Ohio. Obviously, once I had read about the house I went to see it. I had to walk through the woods, which are dark, hardly any sunlight can get through the top of the thickly clustered trees. There is a wall surrounding what is left of the house. I went with my friend Christine and we managed to find a gap in the wall. We went into what must have been the gardens surrounding the house. I saw the coach-houses, which are still standing.

The floor is cobbled and the roof is arched; around the back of the coach-houses there are what looked like little hovels. I don't know if these belonged to the servants or stable-hands. They are pretty run down. We searched around but not much of that part of the house remains. We did not stay too long. I felt a bit uneasy and I did not know if we would be in trouble if it was private property or not.

After my visit to the house I had the dream less frequently. About a year after this I was divorced. I went on living in my own house with the children. My ex-husband would collect the children every Sunday and take them out. One summer Sunday the children went off for the day as usual. When they returned home in the evening my eldest daughter, who was now twelve, told me she had been to see this big old house in Hale. Of course, I was a bit shocked. I asked her why she went there and she said her father knew the man who had bought it and he was trying to renovate it, for what purpose I don't know.

It seems the man had told my ex-husband to call down and he would show him around. So he took the children. My daughter said there was a staircase but it lead nowhere and the walls were crumbling, but mostly the front of the house was standing. She went into the grounds at the back. There was a statue of a girl in the garden. She said they all thought it looked like me. I don't know if this is just their imagination as I have not seen the statue myself. My ex-husband and my children knew nothing about my dreams. I never told them so why they should connect the statue with me is strange.

After my daughter told me about the statue I went back there with my friend and my daughter. I asked her to show us where it was, but the man who had bought it had blocked up the gap in the wall and we could not get in. It was very disappointing. I suppose I could have asked my ex-husband to get permission from his friend to allow me to see it, but I did not want to tell anyone about the dream. I still did not really know what it was about.

As I am reading *The History of Hale*, I find that Sir Gilbert and his wife Margaret died without leaving any children but they were not without heirs. Sir Gilbert had three sisters, Eleanor, Martha and Barbara, and one brother, George. Barbara and George died young. I don't know if the fact that a girl called Barbara lived in the house has anything to do with my dreams of the house. I never really went into that part. After I learned all this information, I stopped having the dream.

I moved house with the children. My ex-husband moved into the house I had given up. After about a year or so he did some work on the house, alterations and so on. The children used to visit each week and one day my daughter came home and said her father had put slate all around the new fireplace. 'It's really lovely, it's all black slate, and he has varnished it.'

The strange thing was, the slate was given to my ex-husband by a friend, the friend being the man who had bought Hale Hall. The slate came from the roof of Hale Hall, and it is now around the fireplace of my old house. My ex-husband does not live there now, and I don't have dreams any more. I don't know what it all means. I don't know why I had those dreams, maybe I should have looked further into it. Hale village still holds a strange fascination for me. I always feel at home there. I still go there on summer days.

Barbara Lee's dream seems to support the externalist view as propounded by Carl Jung. Barbara did not have an insight before about this Hale Hall, so the dream was like a puzzle to her. There was this conflict in her mind until the time after she had seen the house. Dreams bring a message of their own. Our knowledge to this extent is somehow limited. Some dreams are beyond our imagination. But even so the interpreters would have known what these dreams were pointing at. As I see it, the dreamer is a good interpreter. Barbara Lee believes that the little Barbara who had lived at Hale Hall is actually now herself. This belief is further strengthened by the fact that Barbara had a brother who bore the same name as this present Barbara's brother. Besides, the dream went on recurring and stopped only after Barbara had made an effort to see the house.

Barbara took it to mean the dream was actually telling her where she had lived before. Since then her belief in reincarnation has been strengthened. She believes in helping people, and it doesn't have to be people that she knows. For example, she has contributed generously to the plight of Mozambique refugees. Topics such as reborn fortune-telling are among Barbara Lee's interests. As Carl Jung had perceived in his belief in reincarnation, 'When I die my deeds will follow along with me, that is how I imagine it.' She shares the same belief.

Barbara Lee had another, similar reincarnation dream. This dream was not directed to her but to her friend. Thus she writes:

> I was very upset when my friend Irene died. Irene was only Thirty two years old and she was in a wheelchair. She was full of life and didn't want to die. She had a disease called Friedric Ataxia and she suffered greatly. Irene and I had long talks about dying and she knew she did not have very long to live. She asked me if I believed in ghosts. I said I didn't know – I had an open mind about it. She said if she could come back as a ghost, she would appear to me. I said, 'No, Irene, because I would be afraid.' She laughed and said, 'You would not be afraid of me, would you?' I said, 'Yes, so don't do it.' Irene died not long afterwards. I was very upset. For a couple of weeks I was very depressed about her death. I kept thinking of how much she had wanted to live.
>
> I had a dream about Irene not long after she died. In the dream Irene was sitting in her wheelchair, but she looked very happy and very healthy. I felt she could walk. I could see her walk. I could see her long, shiny black hair and her dark-red sweater, which was her favourite one. She looked so happy and well. All she said was, 'I am alright, I am alright,' repeatedly.
>
> The next day I came to work I told my friends and I felt much better. I felt that she was now happy and well, maybe in a better place. Later, Irene's sister came to where I work. I had never met her before. We spoke to each other. She told me how upset she was over Irene. She said that she had had a dream about Irene the previous night and the words she

uttered were, 'I am alright, I am alright.' Immediately I
thought of my own dream. These were the exact words Irene
had said to me in my dream. The sister told me she was
relieved and felt much better to hear her saying that she was
alright, just as I had.

Here were two individuals dreaming about Irene in the stretch of
one night. Yet they had never met before. Their link was Irene.
This dream was reaffirming the existence of transmigration. Both
Barbara and Irene's sister strongly believe Irene is somewhere
alive, and in good spirits. She is 'alright'.

Although I support the externalist theory, there comes a point
where the internalist view of the dream takes over. Barbara and
Irene had a discussion about ghosts before the latter's death. It
seems as if Irene's words were implanted in Barbara Lee's mind,
and she ended up dreaming of it. Irene was near death and
presumably she could see her body from a disembodied perspective, and saw herself moving like a ghost. Probably Irene wanted
encouragement from Barbara, to hear her say, 'Yes, your soul will
enter into a ghost and you will come and live with us again . . .'

It is very interesting for people to have the same dream at the
same time. While Barbara Lee's dream seems to originate from
within, Irene's sister's dream, by contrast, supports the externalist
view. To this end, one could deduce that both Adler and Jung
must be right in this respect, whichever view one takes. What is
critical is the usefulness of the dream in terms of its interpretation
and hence the messages, new messages, it brings. We would like
to believe that some dreams are meaningful and bring a message
which is entirely new.

The idea of ghosts seems to be common. Sometimes people
attribute this to the way the burial was conducted. This supports
what David Christie Murray wrote in his book *Reincarnation,
Ancient Beliefs and modern Evidence*, that a man whose death rites
were not conducted properly might become a ghost and haunt the
living.[16]

Whether people actually experience or see these ghosts is
another matter. But it seems to be a common view. By implication,
if one disputes this ghost idea strange things happen to one. While
I was at theological college in Malawi (1968–70), I shared my views
with other student theologians. I pointed out that I did not believe

in witches or ghosts. Revd. Gande warned me not to mention that again to outsiders. If I did, I would face serious consequences, including confrontation with the ghosts. Or even worse: I could easily find myself in the graveyard. The witches would have done this to me to show that they exist.

There are stories reported about children who talk about their experience during a past life. They experience hallucinations. They can remember living before. My friends at Parkside Hostel in Liverpool in 1989 told me of a programme they watched on BBC2 where children talked about their past life. Some could remember their previous parents and wished to go back to them.

This is difficult to comprehend here, since children do not really know what death is. But with church teachings it is also easy for children to think about the other life. This could be interpreted as being reborn again. When I was a little girl attending Sunday school, I used to have dreams of angels wearing long white robes. My mother interpreted this as indicating righteousness and upright behaviour and said it would guarantee my entry into heaven. Sometimes I used to dream of a white man in shining white robes. My mother would say that's Jesus Christ. But this was utter nonsense. It was only a reflection of the biased racist teachings of the old missionaries, who associated whiteness with righteousness and blackness with evil. This is an indication of how passive the early missionaries' teaching was and how they influenced people's thinking and day-to-day activities.

If I was dreaming of 'non-angelic' activities – for example, people brewing beer – my mother would see it as having changed my ways of living for the devil, or of being under Satanic influence. According to her, the fire was an indication of an immediate punishment from God.

We are also taught that if you grow up as a rude person, upon death and burial the witches would wake you up and start accusing you of all sorts of things. With these in mind some girls fear to marry an outsider. They fear that, if they do, they might not be buried at home when they die. Thus, in dreams while we were children one could actually see those people stigmatised as bad or witches waking you up to interrogate you. This applies to seeing another world and pictures of angels when you are about to die. This kind of teaching is also part of teaching morals or good conduct. It is passed from generation to generation and is taught as a form of legend.

Although what has been discussed above does not really refer to the past life as indicated earlier, the account about life after death could be interpreted by some as proving that they existed before and were reborn, if it is possible to be interrogated after death. This encourages some adults to think they existed before.

A more convincing reincarnation dream comes from Hans Holfer. This story is mentioned by David Christie Murray in *Reincarnation, Ancient Beliefs and Modern Evidence*.

June Volpe, a twenty-nine-year-old Pennsylvanian housewife, went on her first major trip to Silver Springs, Florida. She had a vivid dream of herself as a nineteenth-century 'southern belle' visiting a house she owned. The next day, visiting a haunted house in a local, derelict town, she recognised both as having featured in her dream. She was told that a Mrs Elizabeth Simms had been murdered in the house, shot in the back in 1896, when she was eighty-nine. While Mrs Volpe was in the house she felt as if her body were being moved by some other entity within it. She escaped from the house and, looking back, saw at a window a young girl in a white dress, with long brown hair. When she returned to Pennsylvania her husband noticed a great change in her, almost as if she had become a different person, with some-times a southern accent in her speech.

Regressed in two sessions of hypnosis to fifty years before her birth as June Volpe, she became Mary Elizabeth Tibbits, eighteen-year-old daughter of Frank and Catherine, with a brother Melvin, aged twenty-three, and a grandfather, Gordon, living in Atlanta, Georgia, during the time of President Jackson. She had a boy-friend, Robert Simms, with five children, living at Red Florida. She revealed that her killing was accidental, a rifle catching in the clothes of the supposed assassin. Mrs Simms related how she had communicated with June coming to Red Mill house. She was going to live in June's mind, 'with her, as her'. She spoke of her sons and aspects of her life.[17]

One Zambian man by the name of George Zimba, who was studying at Liverpool University in 1981, told me of an incident involving his grandmother and her brother, who were both mar-ried. It happened that his grandmother had a male child and the brother of his grandmother had a female child. Her brother complained, or had wished that he had a boy baby and his grand-mother also complained saying she wanted a girl.

There was a man in the same village who dreamt these two children were going to die and be reborn again. The man told the grandmother and grandfather not to worry, for they were going to have things in future the way they wanted them. Eventually, the two children died, of course, at different times, but in the same year. In due course George's grandmother conceived again and had a baby girl as she had wanted to. The wife of his grand-mother's brother conceived again, too, and had a male child as the man wished.

How this worked is very strange. George assured me this was a true story. The female child, George confessed, was his mother. The two children experienced reincarnation.

Sylvia Carnston et al., in their book Reincarnation: A New Horizon in Science, Religion and Society, give an account of a girl as recited by a British physicist, Raynor Johnson, in his book A Religious Outlook for Modern Man. He records this girl's dream in her own words.

The dream was of being a prisoner in a place that I knew to be the Tower of London. I had not seen it in real life, but I had no doubt where I was. It was very cold weather (in waking life, a hot summer). I was aware that I had been condemned to death. This I used to dream over and over again, and after being in the dream a vigorous man, to wake me up and be a little girl, felt rather strange.

At last the dream changed and I was standing on a scaffold which must have been newly erected as it smelt of sawdust. Everything was decorous and decent. The executioner knelt and apologised for what he was about to do. I took the axe from his hand and felt it, and handed it back, bidding him do his duty. When I woke up I made a drawing of the axe, which was of a peculiar shape.

Some time after this I asked to be taken to the Tower of London, and I explained to a friendly gunsmith that I wanted to write history but could not understand the battles perfectly until I understood the weapons. 'You are right, missy,' he said, and demonstrated to me the various uses of pike, lace, crossbow, etc. I then asked had he an axe that beheaded people? He said, 'Yes, this certainly beheaded the Jacobite Lords, but it is supposed to be very much older.' Somehow I was not surprised that it proved to be the exact shape of the axe in my dreams.[18]

I could link this with a dream of my own. I used to dream of a strange land with green pastures, valleys, rivers and trees and mountains. Everything was green; the trees had lovely green leaves. I could walk all over along this beautiful land. Everything was strange and unusual. I was always all by myself and the place was so quiet. I used to enjoy the scenery and yet at the same time I was frightened to be on my own. This dream repeated itself for quite a long time.

It only stopped when I came over to Britain and saw the Lake District, in Cumbria, at which point the dream stopped completely. I don't know whether this could mean that I had lived in Cumbria before, but I don't share that view of reincarnation. I believe in resurrection, which is different from reincarnation. Having said this, one could say some places at home (Malawi) could be compared with the Lake District. More confusingly I had a vivid dream while here in Britain. My sister, who died in 1973, was telling me she and her husband had always lived in Britain.

I had an ongoing problem. I dreamt of my sister. She was in a beautiful house with British architecture. Strangely enough she was living in this house with her husband, who is still alive. In this dream there were two of them together, but the yard of the house, the way flowers were arranged, looked also like one of the houses I had seen in Blantyre (Malawi). However, my sister actually spoke to me. She said, 'Why are they troubling you? Don't let anyone trouble you. You are not all by yourself here in Britain. You are with us. We have lived in Britain for a long time, only our house is underground. For this reason people do not see us.' My brother-in-law, Mr Thadzi, talks a lot but on this occasion he was just acknowledging everything my sister was saying. After my sister had finished talking I woke up and was disappointed to learn that it was only a dream.

When I went to Malawi in August 1990, I shared this dream with my uncle from my mother's side. He interpreted the dream to mean the guardian spirits of the dead. We might be somewhere thinking we are on our own when in actual fact the spirits of the dead surround us in times of difficulties.

A friend of mine, Mrs Margaret Chingwanda, who was studying as a nurse, told me she used to dream of a strange land and the dream continued and when she came to Britain she discovered the place she used to dream of was Glasgow. Her husband, a medical doctor, Phil Chingwanda, told me of a similar dream he experienced while in Zimbabwe. He said he used to dream of a strange land and did not know what the dream was telling him. When he came over too, he found that the place he used to dream about was Birmingham.

It is not known whether these dreams wanted to point out something about the future. It is also difficult to associate these dreams with reincarnation. As I have stated earlier, there is a place in Malawi which could look like the Lake District. Apparently there are some places in Zimbabwe which could be compared to the places Phil and Margaret dreamt of. But they were together the day I went to have a chat with them and they asserted with one voice that these were completely strange countries, places they had never seen before.

This chapter has discussed the possibility of dream reincarnation as experienced by Barbara Lee and others. Barbara strangely believes she existed before and, according to her, thinks the Bible also talks about reincarnation when the prophets asked Jesus whether he was Elijah. The death of her friend Irene made her believe that Irene must be living somewhere in another world – a world of the unknown, as some might put it.

A very convincing thing is what Carl Jung wrote on the question of pre-existence, that he existed before and that he was reborn again to finish the unfinished business. He had been an historian before. Like Barbara Lee, Carl Jung believed in transmigration if one lived a good life. Some people also believe in being reborn as an animal if you have lived a bad life.

Chapter 5

Dreams in All Ages

Dreams have been useful in almost every society. They have influenced mankind for centuries, as well as the prophets in the Bible. Prophets listened to the Lord through dreams and knew what the Lord required them to do. Whether we like it or not, dreams have been a real force in the lives of people in all ages. While some have refused to recognise the role of dreams, dreams are used as a guide in most societies, as discussed earlier. Plato in the *Republic* quoted by Nerys Dee (1984) in the book *Your Dreams and What They Mean*, stated: 'In all of us, even in good men, there is a lawless wild beast nature which peers out in sleep.'[1] Brian Inglis, writing in the *Guardian* on 9 September 1987, argued that 'even a hundred rationalists cannot deny the usefulness of dreams.'[2]

In almost every society there are people who are gifted in dream interpretation. In the biblical Old Testament Joseph was treated with great respect in Egypt because of his ability in dream interpretation. Plato was very much respected by the Greeks because he knew the art of dream interpretation. Indeed, references to dreams are found throughout ancient literature, whether carved on the walls of Egyptian temples, in the Bible, or in what is thought to be the oldest dream book of all, compiled by Artemidorus of Ephesus in the second century AD. Dream messages were taken seriously, and every civilised country in the world had its own interpreters or soothsayers.[3] In Africa people had been guided by dreams through the ancestors.

Nerys Dee quotes an old Hittite prayer from long ago, requesting the help of divine powers: 'Either let me see it in a dream or let it be discovered by divination or let a divinely – inspired priestess or priest find out by incubation of a dream whatever it is I demand of them.'[4]

Although Greeks were renowned for their dream interpretation there were before them ancient cultures all over the world who interpreted dreams and made use of them. For example, the Hebrew, Celtic, Arabic, Indian, Chinese, French and Russian cultures all possess ancient records showing the important part dreams played not only in the lives of individuals but in shaping the heritage and destiny of the people as a whole.[5] To some, especially the Greeks, the aim was to know the will of the gods and to receive their divine instructions. People used to seek dreams which would invoke special powers – this was incubation. Those who could dream on behalf of others used to sleep in a sanctuary waiting for a dream reply. It was in a form of ritual and those who practised this abstained from sexual activity, meat-eating and alcohol. They sanctified themselves in order to appear pure in the eyes of the gods.

Greeks believed that they were communicating with their gods through dreams. Many of their sacred shrines were for dream oracles. Those with problems visited the shrine, e.g. Delphi. The shrine of Apollo and the temple of Epidauros are two other famous examples. The sick went to these places hoping to receiving a remedy for their ailments.[6] They believed Asclepius, the god of healing who was known as Imhotep in Egypt, would grant them a revelation during sleep. Ascelpius was an official Greek doctor in whose medical practice dream interpretation played a part. Many philosophers, such as Socrates, dismissed Ascelpius religious ideas, regarding them as a tool of exploitation. The Greeks, on the other hand, recognised 'true' and 'false' dreams. The true ones, as Homer observed, came via the gate of horn, and the false ones via the gate of ivory.

A lot of philosophers have tried to explain the mysteries of sleep and dreams in terms of physical causes. Nerys Dee (1984) mentions that 'Plato, for example, thought that the liver was the seat of dreams but in his famous *Timaeus* he relents by saying that prophetic visions were received by the lower self, through the liver!'[7] Plato here does not distinguish between dreams and visions. Galen, another Greek physician, saw dreams as warnings.

Both Plato and Socrates believed in dreams.

Not long before his death, Socrates told two stories about dreams. He was awaiting the ship from Delphi in order to find out what the oracle called him to do. He dreamt that the ship had arrived and the oracle called him into a spiritual world. He regarded this as an indication of his death. On the last day of his life, he spent time writing poetry because he had dreamt that he should 'make harmony.' At first, he had interpreted this dream as a challenge to become a philosopher, but in this serious moment he had not wanted to risk disobeying his dream and was inclined to write a poem.[8]

Hippocrates described dream as one of the most important methods for diagnosing a patient's illness.[9] A form of hypnotism was universally employed. 'It is clear that endoscopy was highly regarded even by the hard-headed physicians who wrote the Hippocratic treatises: "accurate knowledge of the signs which occur in dreams," one of them claimed, "will be found very valuable for all purposes." '[10] Aristotle also believed that dreams might be used by physicians as an indicator of an ailment or malfunctioning of the body that had not yet manifested itself in outward signs.[11]

The Roman beliefs were similar to those of the Greeks. The Censors took dreams seriously. Calpurnia, wife of Julius Caesar, was supposed to have dreamt of his assassination the night before according to information given by Plutarch. Gustavus Hindman Miller writes: 'If Julius Caesar had been less incredulous about dreams he would have listened to the warning which Calpurnia, his wife, received in a dream.'[12] Artemidorus of Ephesus in the middle of the second century AD made an outstanding contribution to the study of dreams. His work *Onirocritica* (the interpretation of dreams) drew upon much early information and reflected the 'state of the art' in detailed form. He recognised that each person has different associations to dream images and so individual interpretations are necessary. He categorised two classes of dream, the first which he christened 'somnium', which had references to the future, the second which he named 'insomnium', day-dreams.[13]

Equally, the Chinese sage Chuang-tzu (c. 350 BC raised philosophical questions by considering dreams. Thus he wrote: 'Once upon a time, I, Chuang-tzu, dreamt I was a butterfly, fluttering hither and thither, to all intents and purposes a butterfly. I was conscious only of following my fancies as a butterfly and was unconscious of my individuality. Suddenly I was awakened and there I lay, myself again. Now I do not know whether I was a man dreaming I was a butterfly, or whether I am a butterfly now dreaming I am a man.'[14]

Early Christian views and dreaming in the Middle Ages

Although dreams played a significant role in most world societies, they were at one time regarded as taboo. People no longer saw them as a source of inspiration. Influenced by the officials of organised Christian religion, they associated dreams, with other esoteric arts, as devil-inspired. Dream was therefore not seen as a vision but as a forlorn hope.[15] It was under Gregory the Great that Christians began to doubt the importance and value of dream interpretation, although some dream incubation continued into this period. After the Tudor monarchs the role and the power of dreams were almost forgotten. A few Christian writers commented on dreams, but the big problem was to differentiate between divine and demoniacal types.

The early fathers, however, regarded dreams as coming from God as did the people in both the Old Testament and the New, as we shall see in Chapter 6. One of the most interesting cases is that of Polycarp. He dreamt while on his way to Rome that he was going to be killed. This was later fulfilled.[16]

Most of the early Christians suffered great persecution. Their only hope was to look to God for help through dreams. Nearly all of them believed that dreams and visions were the only way of communicating with God. Irenaeus, who lived in Gaul, said that the dream was a means for him to maintain a proper contact with God.[17] Origen, probably the most educated man of his time, wrote many books on dreams in which he emphasised the meaning of the visions of the Old Testament and stressed that every intelligent person regards the dream as a possible means of revelation.[18] Gregory of Nyssar, in the fourth century AD, accepted dreams a divine messages, and even believed them to be mirrors of the soul, which reflected the personality of the dreamer. Thus he wrote in his book 'On Making Man' that from these visions it was possible to better understand and value one's true self.[19] St Augustine (354–430) thought dreams were an important tool for 'grasping both the inner workings of the mind of man and his relationship with God'. His own conversion was foretold in his mother's dream.[20]

Jerome, a contemporary of Augustine, was, while young, entranced with the intellectual excellence of the classics, to such an extent that he preferred them to the Bible. He became seriously ill, and a dream reversed his direction. He dreamt he was before the judgment seat and was condemned for being a 'follower of Cicero and not of Christ'. He suffered excruciating torture and mental torment, culminating in a vow never again to read 'worldly books.'[21] Tertullian, the famous Carthaginian thinker, wrote: 'Is it not known to all the people that the dream is the most usual way that God reveals himself to men?'[22]

The appearance of *The Interpretation of Dreams*, by Freud, in 1911 made people start respecting dreams. The psychologists showed much interest in them.

Historical dreams

Alexander the Great dreamt that the city of Tyros was under siege, and that a Satyros, a native spirit danced on his shield. His personal dream interpreter, Aristander, translated it as a play on words by dividing up and re-arranging the letters in 'satyros' and encouraged Alexander by revealing that Tyros was his. With this interpretation Alexander renewed his attack on the city and the inhabitants surrendered.[23]

Adolf Hitler had a dream in 1917, when the German and French forces were facing each other across the Somme, locked in a deadly artillery bombardment. In his nightmare he saw debris and molten earth descend crushingly and suffocatingly upon him. He got up and dashed outside into the cold night air, to discover it was only a bad dream. A French shell landed on the bunker he had just left and killed all the sleeping occupants.[24] He thanked God for saving his life. He added that he knew he had been rescued so that one day he could in turn save the Fatherland. Probably Europe and the world would have been different now if Hitler had not had this dream.

Napoleon, on the other hand, who saved France, used his dreams to plan his military campaigns. Bismarck was six years old when Napoleon died. He had a prophetic dream which he experienced during his childhood and early military career. He wrote a letter to Emperor William in which he stated: 'Your Majesty's communication encouraged me to relate a dream I had in the Spring of 1863 during the worst of the days of struggle. I dreamt that I was riding on a narrow alpine path, a precipice on my right and rocks to my left. The path grew narrower until my horse refused to proceed. It was impossible to turn round or dismount, so with my whip in my hand I struck the smooth rock and called on God. The whip grew to an enormous length, the rock face dropped like a piece of stage scenery and opened out into a broad path with a view over the hills and forest like a landscape in Bohemia; there were Prussian troups with banners and even in my dream the thought came to me that I must report it to your Majesty.'[25]

This dream inspired Bismarck and he decided to stick with his policies. He then succeeded in Prussia and became leader of the German federation, so paving the way for Hitler's Fatherland. Looking at these dreams, one would say the world would have been different today if these dreamers had not acted upon intuitive insight.

The Egyptians had Pharaohs, who respected their dreams. Their contents were interpreted so as to bestow a divine endorsement on their rulers, and protection upon them and their royal line of successors.

Shakespeare was probably the greatest dreamer of all times. Coleridge insisted in his lectures on Shakespeare that the only way to understand the Bard's message was to interpret his plays as one would a series of images and ideas created and embodied in a dream.[26]

In The Tempest, Caliban dreamt that 'the Isle is full of noises and sounds and sweet airs that give delight and hurt not,' and he cries to dream. The character of the wise man Prospero suggests that life is but a dream. 'We are such stuff as dreams are made of and our life is rounded with little sleep.' The tragedy of Macbeth sees Lady Macbeth taking to sleep-walking, re-enacting her crimes and thus revealing that she possesses at least a grain of conscience. And she is reminded that 'sleep is the balm for hurt minds, nature's great second course.'[27]

Although I have given the account above to witness the usefulness of dreams, some people still doubt the efficiency of dreams.

They think dreams are rubbish or illogical. Some people are under the impression that the dream dominates our inefficient minds during sleep. In 1900 Sigmund Freud gave a certain scientific credibility to dreams when he published *The Interpretation of Dreams*, dispelling doubts in many people's minds. Even then dreams remained relatively neglected, especially in Western countries, where they are still seen as pathological or even simply as an African phenomenon.

In 1982 I was teaching at St Colm's College in Edinburgh. Most of the church ministers were preparing to travel to Third World countries and were interested in some aspects of African culture, and the question of dreams was raised. Nearly everyone in that group said dreams did not exist: they only occur to African people, the group said. There was, however, one minister who supported dreams and was surprised by this dismissive attitude. He said, 'How could we say that to dream is an African phenomenon when it happens even to us.' He was a church minister in his early forties. He himself dreamt of his father's death, which happened in the same year.

However, as stated earlier, history is to some extent threaded with incidents of dream prophecy, be it profane or sacred. Our main interest is that dreams have been useful all through and have influenced both rich and poor in all ages. Dreams, as I see it, will continue guiding and warning people. Thus, people dream now in the same way as they did ages ago. Let us examine the contemporary dreams.

Josie Atkinson, married, with grown-up children, one a lecturer in science at Manchester University, is now in the caring profession. She describes her dream as clear and vivid, the most vivid dream she has ever had. She had this dream on 25 January 1990. She dreamt of a funeral and was with Pat Georgeson at the funeral. Pat works with Josie. There was no one at the funeral except Josie and Pat. A man came on the scene with a camera, wanting to take their photos. Josie and Pat told the man that by its culture it was not permissible to take photos at funerals.

Since there was no one else yet at the funeral, Pat and Josie decided to go for a drink first while waiting for the others to come. They came back and found a few more people had arrived. Later on Josie – still dreaming – saw her little grandson dying. The baby was then eighteen months old. At first they did not know whose funeral it was, then she realised. She was puzzled as to what was happening. She did not realise it was a dream. She thought it was real. Eventually she got up, around 9.00 a.m.; she did not know how to interpret that dream.

At 1.30 p.m. her son came with a baby, at 1.55 p.m. the baby had severe convulsions. Josie called an ambulance while at the same time trying first-aid. She put a wet towel on the child's mouth and pulled the tongue.

The ambulance came and took the child to the hospital. They managed to save the child's life. The doctor said it was not meningitis, as the family had thought, but an infection in the lungs and bowel. The doctor said the baby would have died if they hadn't pulled out his tongue.

This was in a way a warning dream. Since the dream was in the morning, it was telling Josie what was going to happen the same day in the afternoon. This came as a shock to Josie, since she did not expect this to happen. The dream definitely had a message, which was unknown to Josie. When this incident happened Josie knew what the dream was saying to her. This dream supports the externalist view.

Dream premonition

Barbara, to whom I have referred in Chapter 4, had another interesting dream, which she narrates:

In 1972, when I had my first child I dreamt that when I was about six months pregnant my baby would be a girl. I could see her with a lot of hair on her head, a very pretty face, with a little button nose, and a little, well-shaped chin. In the dream she was dressed in a gold yellow-and-white crochet suit. I told my husband and he said, 'Oh, it's just a dream. I am sure you will have a boy.' But I knew. I had seen my baby. I had no doubt at all.

When she was born and they put her in my arms she was exactly as I had seen her. My mother brought a little suit when she was a few weeks old. She did not know about my dream, because I shared it only with my husband. It was a golden yellow-and-white crocheted suit. When I put it on my little girl, the picture was complete. There she was, just as she had appeared in my dream.

Freud would have concluded that the dream was a wish-fulfilment. It seems as if Barbara wanted a girl and could visualise what the child was going to look like. Equally the husband might have wanted a boy, which was why he pointed out that Barbara was going to have a baby boy. The dream is a predictive one. Barbara was already pregnant and she would not have been wanting a child since she knew she was already going to have one.

According to her she would have loved to please the husband and have a boy but she dreamt of and had a baby girl. Dream is real. It tells us about the future and it does not lie.

A girl eighteen years of age, Pollar, dreamt her mattress was torn. When she woke, there was a big cut in the middle of it.

A lady – Mrs H. V. Chapman, who is in her fifties – dreamt some years ago that she and her husband and three small children were living in rooms: they occupied the sitting-room and one bedroom of a house which belonged to an old lady called Mrs Wyne. This elderly lady was very difficult to live with as she was suffering from senile dementia.

Mrs Chapman and the family were desperate to get out of this accommodation, and Mrs Chapman felt that she would have lived in the worst part of Liverpool if only they had a house or a flat of their own.

One night she dreamt of a particular small, terraced house, which was quite near to where they lived. This house had never entered her thoughts while she was awake. In the dream she was looking through the windows of this house – sort of peeping into the interior of the house. She didn't give this dream another thought until six months later, when her friend June came to visit her and told her that her mum could get them a house if they were interested. Interested: that was the understatement of the decade.

That evening Ted, her husband, and she went to see Mrs Blackhurst – June's mother. She informed them that a couple were buying this house off her, and had run into financial difficulties. She was quite prepared to let them rent it. She informed them that the couple in question would be happy to let them see the house there and then. She then told them the address – and to Mrs Chapman's utter disbelief, it was the very house of her dream.

They duly went, and were shown around this compact little house. It was like Buckingham Palace to them. Could this be true? They thought they were in heaven.

About six weeks later, they had started to pack up their belongings in anticipation of their move to their new home, when June came to visit them again. Her mum had come too. They did not look very happy, and the reason for this soon became clear. The couple who had shown them around their little house had overcome their financial difficulties and were not going to vacate the premises. Mrs Chapman and the family were absolutely devastated, and did not ever go to live in that house. Was this, she wondered, why in her dream she was looking through the windows of the house? She did not get inside the house in her dream, and she never went to live there.

Perhaps Freud could receive credit here with his theory of a dream as a wish-fulfilment. It seems to me that Mrs Chapman had this dream since she really wanted to have a house. The thought of the house never departed from her mind or thoughts.

One afternoon in January 1990, I was walking along London Road in Liverpool. I had just been at the central library and decided to have a walk. I was carrying a book on dreams. I entered a post office opposite T. J. Hughes's shop. A lady saw me carrying the book. She called me over. She was selling some other things in the post office, such as biscuits, sweets and soft drinks. She was not on the counter selling stamps, but they have a section where they sell such things. However, she asked me whether I knew how to interpret dreams. I told her I did with some dreams but not all of them. At home in Malawi, I told her, we grow up interpreting dreams.

The lady was somehow worried: I could see it in her. She told me she had a recurring dream every night, and could not sleep. Each night she saw her mother, who had died, appearing to her. The mother said, 'I have come to stay with you.' The lady answered her, saying,' No, mum, you cannot stay with me; you died a long time back.' This dream was continually repeated, so frequently that at each nightfall she worried about what she was going to experience.

I told her that it was difficult to interpret that dream, since the mother did not bring any message apart from saying she wanted to stay with her. I told the lady, however, that at home when those who died appeared to us in a dream, that meant they were not happy with our way of conduct or behaviour. I told her if I was in her position I would try to examine myself and see what evil I was doing, because the ancestors normally came to warn us of something. The lady looked much happier when I said this. She told me she knew what was wrong, and that she was going to try to put it right.

One of the staff at my place of work, Thelma Gordon, was one month pregnant when her grandmother died. No one knew she was pregnant except her grandmother. The grandmother died before she would tell anyone. Thelma, for some reason, did not tell anyone that she was pregnant.

In due course the baby was born. That same night, Thelma had a dream in which her grandmother did not say anything, but just looked at her.

I told her the grandmother had come to congratulate her for having a baby. It could also be that she knew Thelma had a baby and wanted her to know that she was well aware and that she was alive somewhere.

Barbara Garwell – who lives in North Humberside with her husband, Roland – has experienced many premonitions, one of them involving President Sadat of Egypt. Hearne (1989) writes about Barbara's premonition:

> In the dream a sort of stadium was seen, with a simple row of seated men all wearing dark pin-stripe suits. The men had 'coffee-coloured' skin. Barbara knew that sand was nearby and that the setting was somewhere in the Middle East. Two soldiers, also 'coffee-coloured', were observed to go up to the row of men and spray them with automatic fire.' Barbara shared the dream with her husband. Three weeks later, on 6 October 1981, President Anwar Sadat of Egypt was assassinated.[28]

A workmate Sue MacGuire, a development Officer, had a dream before the Gulf War, which I interpreted to mean the war was definitely going to break out. She writes:

I dreamt I was in an office building, not the one I actually
work in, though I seemed to be working there. Some soldiers
came in (they may not have been actually dressed as soldiers
but they were aggressive, authoritative, etc., so I perceived
them as such). I had to give them a child who was a baby,
younger than my youngest, but in some way it wasn't quite
him. I gave the baby reluctantly to them and was upset. My
colleagues did nothing and expressed no feelings about it.
Later on I was hiding a child from the same men. It was my
own eldest child, four years old at the time, but he was again
younger in the dream – two or three. To hide him I had to
put him out on a very dangerous old iron fire escape. I was
very afraid of him wandering off the platform (it was very
high up) but I knew that if I gave him over he would be
killed. After that I had to give him directions to go to a
place of safety and I remember thinking how dangerous and
difficult it was for a child of two or three to follow directions
to get somewhere. The idea that this was a situation which
had arisen out of an outbreak of war in the Gulf was implicit
throughout the dream but it happened before the war.

It was easy for me to interpret the dream because normally women
hide children during war. They would rather die themselves so
long as the children are safe. We used to hide in Mozambique in
1953 when they started fighting for independence in Malawi. Each
time we were running away everyone in the family could remember looking for me, since I was the youngest. Both my mother
and my sisters would look for me. They would not start running
until I was actually there with them.

It was equally easy for me to interpret Sue's dream because I
myself have had two similar dreams. In early September 1990 I
dreamt one British soldier was shooting my brother and my
brother was running away. At the end of the very same month I
had the same dream. This time the British soldier was shooting at
me. I did the same thing as my brother, running away, but still
the soldier would not leave me. He continued pointing the gun
at me. With this dream I knew there was going to be war. When
Sue started telling me of her dream, I said straight away, before
she had even finished telling me, that 'this is definitely war, Sue'.

A colleague had a dream on 30 May 1991. He dreamt he opened

the bathroom door and found the room was full of water. The dream could be interpreted by the fact that his aunt rang the following Saturday, telling him that her bathroom had been flooded. The whole room was full of water, not just the floor. Freud, with his theory of dream as wish-fulfilment, is discredited here. Dream comes of its own accord. Jane Ferguson, in the *Guardian* of 26 April 1989, also pointed out that we dream of things which we do not know about.

Dreaming the opposite

There are some people who dream about the opposite. It does not necessarily mean that the dream was wrong if it does not happen. Even if the dream goes opposite there is still an element of revealing the future. The dream still turns out to be useful if there is a good interpreter. One of our colleagues at work, Emily Hendrick, had two similar dreams early in 1989. She dreamt her husband had died. During the following week she dreamt again that her son John had died. She looked very worried.

I told her what she dreamt was the opposite: both her husband and son were going to live long lives. Though I told her this she still looked very worried, as though she did not believe me. Despite me telling her what the dream meant, she went on explaining to me about these two dreams. She did not believe me, I could see that. However, I assured her that they were not going to die. And I still maintain they will both live long lives.

Another lady, Josephine McManaman, had a dream which gave the opposite meaning. She writes:

When I was a young teenager I decided that love and marriage was not for me. In my early thirties I started thinking, was I doing the right thing? Should I get married or should I not? One night I had a dream, I was in a beautiful white dress, a real bride's dress, but in the church there was no sign of my father and as I walked slowly down the aisle I could see what were almost certainly all my friends and relations standing in the pews. The church was packed. As I reached the altar there was no one there, no priest, no one. This dream told me it was not to be. I am in my early fifties and still unmarried.

Mr Stan Ruddock is in his late seventies. He used to have a recurring dream. Each time he would dream of drowning in the sea and ended up fearing water. He had a girlfriend the other time and his girlfriend had the same dream. She dreamt of him drowning. She shared her dream with Stan and Stan told her he had had that same dream several times before, while a little boy, and the same dream still continued.

While in middle age Stan went to work in Japan, and there he fell in a river. He tried to swim near the banks of the river, trying to get a grip on something which could save his life but there was nothing he could get hold of. A ship saw him and picked him up. That was a reality of his dream. Since then Stan has never had that dream again. Although his fears have gone, Stan still thinks he will die in water. He thinks the dream was revealing how he is going to die, a belief reinforced by the fact that his girlfriend had the same dream.

Brian Inglis, writing on the opposites, once said, 'I grew up accepting certain prevalent assumptions about dreams. If they meant anything, they went by opposites: to dream of failing an examination presaged passing it.'[29]

In Malawi there are people whose dreams are only about the opposite. For example, if someone is sick in a village with a sickness which worries everyone and takes away their peace and they dream he is dead, that means he will not die. This kind of dream brings a message of happiness or comes to strengthen people. Whoever has this kind of dream goes round sharing the dream he has had with others. He does that in order that people can start going to the fields. Normally people do not go to the fields when someone is very sick.

Day-dreaming

Dreams do not necessarily have to come during sleep. They occur, too, when one is wide awake, as was the case with Mary Duggan. Mary is in the caring profession. She is fifty-three. She shared her dream with me. She was standing by a staircase at her house. She encountered her mother, who had died a long time before. The mother was beckoning to her. Mary wondered what it was all about. She thought it was real seeing her mother, but discovered she was only day-dreaming.

My mother told me of a similar incident. One day, as she was sitting in the kitchen, her sister, who had died several years before appeared to her. She saw her standing outside by a pillar. My mother wondered if her sister had come back to life. She actually went to check outside where her sister was standing, only to realise she had been day-dreaming.

Keith Hearne, in *Visions of the Future* (1990), states that this imaging process of wakefulness is probably the same one that operates in dreams. He further argues that we have no reason to separate the two.[30]

In another private discussion, Dr Themba Chumbe, a medical practitioner from Zimbabwe but practising in England, told me a startling story of what happened to him and a friend of his while driving. He could visualise a puncture in the tyre. He told his friend. They stopped and checked, but did not find any puncture. His friend asked him what made him think there had been a puncture. He did not know what to say. But certainly he was embarrassed. He apologised and they continued their journey.

However, no sooner had they finished this discussion than the car swerved and came to an abrupt stop. The two men got out to check what had gone wrong. They discovered it was a tyre puncture and this implied a big hole in the tyre. So after all there was a puncture. This is the kind of thing Keith Hearne would describe as 'premonitions appearing to the percipients as day visions'.[31]

In early 1977 I was supposed to go to Zambia to study at Mindolo Ecumenical Foundation. Before I went I was troubled at heart. I did not know what was bothering me. My mother had a brother, the only one she had. I was very fond of him. I did not see him for quite a long time, since we were living in separate places. Originally my mother was from Gowa, where my uncle still lived. She moved to Lizulu to join my father when they got married. It was difficult to get to Gowa from Lizulu. The nearest bus stage was a distance away. Moreover, it was rumoured that there were people hiding in the thick forests separating Gowa from the main roads, which were therefore risky for young girls to travel on alone.

However, my uncle kept on appearing to me during the day. This happened almost every day before I left for Zambia. I asked my sister Inesi to escort me to Gowa. She refused on the grounds of lack of money. I offered to pay her fare. She still could not be persuaded, citing the dangers of the forest. My uncle kept on appearing to me. I went to Lilongwe to stay with a friend of mine, Hannah Mabasa, headmistress of Lilongwe Girls' Secondary School at that time. I told her of my wish to visit my uncle. She discouraged me, arguing that it was not safe to make such trips when I was preparing for a major journey to Zambia. Anything can happen during such short trips which might spoil my journey. I had no choice but to give up the whole idea of going to see my uncle.

Even then I did not have peace of mind. In February 1977 I started off on my journey to Zambia. It was only for a short course, six months on women's leadership. Not long into the course, probably in March, I received a letter from my sister saying that my uncle had died. This is consistent with Keith Hearne's argument that in all societies, great and small, there is a belief that under certain circumstances the future can be revealed.

This chapter has tried to show how dream had conditioned and influenced people of all ages, generations, nationalities and races. I have shown how dreams from the time of Plato to the present day have affected people both rich and the poor, strong and weak. Dreams appear to have been considered important in several ancient societies. Although the Greeks were renowned for their dream interpretation, there were other cultures all over the world, such as the Egyptians and the Hebrews, who also knew how to interpret dreams. I have shown how people were guided by dreams in choosing their careers, e.g. Socrates. The early fathers, too, regarded dreams as coming from God in the same way as peoples of both the Old and New Testaments have believed. I have also shown that dream plays a very important role today. People are still trying to interpret their dreams.

Although dreams were regarded as important, in the Middle Ages they were linked with sorcery by officials of Christianity. However, dream incubation persisted into this period. The problem was, however, how to distinguish between the profane and the sacred. With the appearance of Freud's *The Interpretation of Dreams*, people began debating dreams again. I have also shown how day-dreaming can predict the future. Some dreams I have shown go by the opposites.

Chapter 6

Biblical Dreams

Most ancient societies regarded dreams as a channel of communication between this world and the next. Archaelogists have discovered information about Babylonian and Assyrian beliefs from the great library at Nineveh (5000 BC). Both the Assyrian and the Babylonian societies tried to interpret dreams. For example dreaming of flying indicated disaster for the dreamer.[1]

One of the oldest recorded dreams is to be found in Mesopotamian literature, prophesising an impending disaster.[2] The person who had this dream described a huge tidal wave engulfing and swamping much of the face of the earth.[3] The dream relates to the biblical account of the flood. The oldest dream book in the world is thought to be a collection of Assyrian, Babylonian and Egyptian dream lore called Artimedorus' *Onirocritica*.[4]

In Babylonia Manu was the goddess of dreams. Temples were erected and dedicated to her, and magical rites were conducted to counter devils and spirits of the dead, especially those which caused unpleasant dreams.

The ancient Egyptians, too, believed that dreams were messages from the gods. This is also true of contemporary African belief, as already discussed in Chapter 3.

The interpretation of dreams has to make allowance for origin and content, and also take into consideration the understanding of human psychology and the 'world view' of the people involved.

Hippocrates said, 'some dreams are divinely inspired but others are the direct result of the physical body'.[5] I am inclined to agree with Hippocrates here. There are some dreams which come from God and some which are the result of the physical body, with the addition that the latter are from the devil. I am more and more inclined to think that in everything there is the 'sacred' and the 'profane'. Like Hippocrates, Francis Crick also believes that dreams are messages from the Gods. Brian Inglis, on the other hand, in his book *The Power of Dreams*, said: 'Not all that people see in them comes true; for there are two gates, one of horn, and the other of ivory.' Inglis is here just putting it in a different way.[6]

The problem is that there are some people whose dreams, whatever they are always come true. I call this the realisation rate (RR). There are equally some people whose dreams do not become true. These I have coined 'zero RR'. A friend of mine who was the first female lawyer in Malawi and is now living in Ivory Coast came to to London in 1989. She is of the contention that dreams are from the devil, they have zero RR and they come to frighten us. This may be true, but it represents only one side of the story. There are dreams which are divinely inspired. All the dreams I have experienced are informative as well as prophetic. My RR can therefore be said to be very high. My dreams predict actual events. Thus, they occur for a specific purpose.

Equally, that there should be divine dreams was also doubted by Aristotle. On the other hand, St Augustine believed demons could to some extent affect dreams. He asked God in his prayer to maintain him in 'chaste desire' in sleep and protect him from bad dreams or from dreams which would result in pollution.[7]

Gustavus Hindman Miller accepts the notions of profane and sacred. He asserts that, whether profane or sacred, history is threaded with incidents of dream prophecy. Ancient history relates that Gennadius was convinced of the immortality of his soul by conversing with an apparition in his dream. It was also through the dream of Cecilla Metella, the wife of a consul, that the Roman Senate was induced to order the temple of Juno Sospita to be rebuilt[8].

Biblical dreams

Dreams were treated with great respect. There are some 130 references to dreams, and almost 100 to visions, in the Bible.[9] Dreams played a very important role and carried value in the emerging church, as both the beginning of the Gospel story and the strategy of growth and evangelism depended to some extent upon responding to dreams and visions.[10] That the Bible is full of dreams shows that God does certainly communicate with those whom He loves through dreams. God touches people's lives through the prophetic and written word; by the wonder of nature; by His mighty acts of deliverance; and also by dreams.

There were those prophets, such as Daniel, Jeremiah and Ezekiel, in particular, who were noted for their dreams. Whatever one dreamt was interpreted and action was taken. When Gideon went to war to fight the Medianites and during the night went on a spying mission into the enemy camp, he arrived just as one man was narrating a dream to a fellow soldier. Gideon was interested and listened intently. Thus the dream went: 'I had a dream, a round loaf of barley bread came tumbling into the Medianite camp. It struck the tent with such force that the tent overturned and collapsed.'[11] His friend interpreted it to mean that it was nothing but the sword of Gideon, son of Joash, the Israelite.

When Gideon heard the dream and its interpretation, he worshipped God. He returned to the camp of Israel and called out, 'Get up: The Lord has given the Midianite camp into your hands.' (Judges 7, v. 15, NIV). With this information we can see how God can communicate with His people through dreams.

Another good example is that of Jacob. Jacob was a great dreamer among the Patriarchs. In his dream he realised God was with him at Bethel. He saw a ladder set up on earth, extending to heaven, and angels were ascending and descending it. The Lord stood above it and said, 'I am the Lord, the God of Abraham your father and the God of Isaac. The land on which you lie will be given to you and your descendants shall be like the dust of earth, and you shall spread abroad to the West and East and to the North and the South; and by you and your descendants shall all the families of the earth bless themselves. Behold, I am with you and will keep you wherever you go, and will bring you back to this land; for I will not leave you until I have done that of which I have spoken to you.' (Gen. 28 v. 12–17).

In terror Jacob recognised that the place was God's house, earth's entrance into heaven. He set up the stone as a pillar and annointed it with oil. This stone was presumably the most sacred object in the later sanctuary. Jacob therefore vowed that in return this stone should be God's house.

The narrative reflects ancient ideas that saw earth and heaven as close together, connected by a stairway, with heaven's gate at the foot. The angels were not winged, like the seraphim or the cherubim, and therefore needed the stairway.

The stone was the house of God, as Jacob learned from the dream. It was a widespread belief that certain stones were inhabited by deity. It was also a custom for the people to sleep out in sanctuaries so that they might receive oracles in their dream. Jacob practised 'incubation' unintentionally. He shuddered at his involuntary trespass on sacred ground.

However, while Jacob was asleep Yahweh revealed himself by his name and promised him the land, personal protection, and safe return. In this dream God showed Jacob his destiny. He told him about his future, that his descendants were going to multiply like sand. Von Frang, the foremost Jungian analyst, as Jane Ferguson reports in the *Guardian*, 4 April 1989, believes dreams show us 'how to find meaning in our lives, how to fulfil our destiny'.

I am sure Jacob was relieved after his dream. No doubt he was afraid to travel by himself. But God showed him his destiny and promised to go before him. He assured him that he was going to protect him. Surely in my mind a dream is to some extent a religious experience. God reveals Himself to people through dreams. When Jacob awoke from his sleep he said, 'Surely the Lord is in this place, and I did not know it.' (Gen. 28, vs. 16–17, RSV).

Jacob made a vow and promised to serve God. He understood God's nature in his dream. It is only if one is capable of understanding the dream that one can know its meaning and nature. While some dreams are from the devil, as others believe, some are from God, as we have seen. God reveals himself to the people through dreams and some people have actually given themselves to God because of their dreams. Indeed, the subject of dream plays a great part in the biblical narrative.

As a great dreamer, Jacob had another dream experience, in which he wrestled with an angel in the night at the brook Jabbok. In this dream Jacob was wounded in the struggle. His name was changed to Israel. God said to him, 'No longer shall your name be called Jacob, but Israel shall be your name'. (Gen. 35, v. 10, RSV) Apparently God changed Jacob's name in order to make him a new man altogether. It was a sort of purification. Jacob, however, learned through this dream that some sort of transformation was needed in him and his lameness remained as a reminder of this dream experience.

The significance of this dream is that Jacob had a new name, Israel. It was like purifying him since he was in a land where people worshipped idols. Although Jacob still worshipped God, he was to some extent unclean in the eyes of God. His lameness was also an indication of making him a completely different person. 'This second appearance is a fulfilment of the promise made in the former; and the second pillar is a testimony that the faith and hope indicated by the former have been justified by the event.'[12]

Dreams also have the effect of warning, such as happened with Joseph. Joseph had two dreams which referred to his greatness. He said to his brothers, 'Hear this dream which I have dreamt, behold, we were binding sheaves in the field, and lo, my sheaf arose and stood upright and behold your sheaves gathered round it and bowed to my sheaf.' (Gen. 37, vs. 6–7, RSV) His brothers hated him and asked whether Joseph was really going to rule and have dominion over them.

In the second dream Joseph saw the sun, the moon and eleven stars bowing down to him. Although Joseph knew his brothers hated him for telling the first dream, he could not keep the second dream secret and revealed it to them. His brothers' hatred increased. On hearing the dream his father asked Joseph, 'What is this dream that you have dreamt? Shall I and your mother and your brothers indeed come to bow ourselves to the ground before you?' (Gen. 37, v. 10) But although Joseph's father questioned Joseph's dreams he kept their meaning in his heart.

Joseph's story would have been difficult to follow without his dream interpretation. It is therefore true to say that his dreams exalted him above all members of his family. He interpreted while in prison the dream of the butler and the baker of the King of Egypt. And Joseph's interpretations became true. When the butler and the baker had their dreams they looked sad, since they did not know what their dreams meant. Joseph made it clear to them that dream interpretation belonged to God (Gen 40).

The chief butler told his dream to Joseph, and said to him: 'In my dream there was a vine before me, and on the vine there were three branches; as soon as it budded, its blossoms shot forth, and the clusters ripened into grapes. Pharaoh's cup was in my hand

and I took the grapes and pressed them into Pharaoh's hand.' Joseph interpreted this dream to mean the butler was going to go back to Pharaoh's chamber and start working again. Joseph told him to remember him.

Seeing how Joseph interpreted the butler's dream, the baker told him his dream as well. 'I also had a dream: there were three cake-baskets on my head and in the uppermost basket there were all sorts of baked food for Pharaoh, but the birds were eating it out of the basket on my head.' (Gen. 40, vs. 16–17, RSV) Joseph answered and told him that within three days Pharaoh was going to lift up the baker's head and hang him on a tree to be eaten by the birds.

All that Joseph had told the butler and the baker came true; it follows, then, that a dream is a reflection of truth; it does not lie.

It is also very interesting to note that dreams were sometimes repeated in the Bible until the dreamt-of action had actually taken place. Pharaoh's dream of the years of abundance and famine was repeated until after Pharaoh had taken some action. Pharaoh was greatly troubled by this dream, which many people tried to interpret, but Pharaoh was not satisfied. The butler then remembered Joseph and told Pharaoh about him. Pharaoh ordered Joseph to come out of prison. Joseph interpreted the dream to Pharaoh. Joseph told him there was going to be seven years of abundance and seven years of famine. Pharaoh was satisfied with the interpretation and put him in charge of organising and keeping the food.

As it was, Joseph became ruler over the land of Egypt. His brothers came to buy corn and Joseph recognised them. He first treated them badly to see whether their hearts had changed. Later Joseph was convinced that love and forgiveness may have free course.

The brothers went back to Jacob, their father, and fulfilled Joseph's dreams. Later on Pharaoh invited Joseph's family to Egypt. Both the brothers and Jacob, his father, went down to Egypt and Joseph looked after them. People from other parts of the world went, too, during the seven-year period of famine.

As I have stated above, we can see that God was with Joseph from the very beginning. His brothers hated him for telling the truth. God liked Joseph because he was a man who could tell the truth and did not fear anything. God is here linked with the truth.

Jesus said, 'I am the way, the truth and the life.' (John 14, v. 6, RSV) Whatever he had experienced, he could not hide it. God actually communicated with Joseph through dreams and told him about his future greatness and destiny. Joseph feared God for the rest of his life and God blessed him for that. Indeed, he was imprisoned because he did not want to displease God, and be forced to commit sin. God, however, guided him and directed him all through, having chosen him from among his brothers.

Parker (1988) argues that dreams are a gift from a living God and they are intended for our good. They come from God, who loves us and makes Himself known to us. He is loving and wants to protect His children by warning them through dreams. Dreams come to us to tell us something we were not aware of, to open our eyes and to warn us of any danger which is ahead of us. They direct and correct us. They are very useful indeed, although they tell us even what we do not want to hear or face up to.

In the New Testament dreams have an authoritative role. It was a dream which made Joseph tolerate Mary's pregnancy. In another dream the Lord told Joseph to escape to Egypt and Joseph and Mary did as the dream commanded them. The dreams are used in this way in order to encourage us or strengthen us in a thing we are disinclined at first to do. The dreams are used in this way to bring understanding of something we are not clear about. They are used in this way so that we should not ignore the thing which God has proved to be right. It is also very interesting to learn that the wise men were told in a dream not to return to Herod. If they had, something would probably have happened to the young boy, Jesus. So dreams are also used in order to protect us, and to warn us of the danger which is in front of us.

Visions

Visions are closely paralleled by dreams. Parker (1988) demonstrated that visions and dreams are at some level identical experiences. He adds that they all are similar moments, except that dreams are usually the creation of the dreamer and provide an avenue for God to enter into dialogue with the individual. Visions are given by God and the content is not influenced by the sleeper.[13]

It is worth mentioning here that any spiritual experience is bound to involve emotions, yet it does not necessarily follow that the individual has lost his sense of reason and objectivity. Peter's experience on the rooftop at Joppa is relevant here.

The apostle Peter, while he was hungry and while the meal was being prepared, fell into a trance. He saw the heaven open and something descending, like a great sheet let down by its four corners. It contained all kinds of four-footed animals, as well as reptiles of the earth and birds of the air. A voice came to him: 'Rise Peter, kill and eat.' But Peter said 'No, Lord, for I have never eaten anything that is common or unclean.' The voice came to him a second time: 'What God has cleansed you must not call common.' This happened three times and the thing was taken up to heaven. (Acts 10, vs. 9–16, RSV)

While Peter was contemplating what the vision might have meant, three men asked for him. Peter went to meet the men and told them he was the one they were asking for. 'Cornelius, a centurion, an upright and God-fearing man, who was well spoken of by the whole Jewish nation, was directed by a holy angel to send for you to come to his house, and to hear what you have to say'[14] said the men. Peter accompanied the men and went with 'hem to Caesarea.

We see in this vision that the apostle was commanded to eat food which his traditional Judaism classified as unclean and he would strongly have refused. But the vision had to recur, telling Peter the very same thing. This helped Peter face up to his prejudices towards the Gentiles. In this sense the vision had commanded Peter to do that thing which he would not have done on his own.

In the Old Testament, Isaiah the Prophet had a vision. He saw the Lord sitting on a throne and above him stood the seraphim. Each had six wings; with two he covered his face and with two he covered his feet, and with two he flew. The seraphim praised God: 'Holy, holy, holy is the Lord of hosts.' The house was filled with smoke; having seen the Lord, Isaiah cried that he was 'unclean'; one of the seraphim flew to Isaiah with a burning coal which he had taken with tongues from the altar, and touched Isaiah's lips and told him his guilt was taken away. Isaiah heard the voice of the Lord: 'Whom shall I send, and who will go for us?' Isaiah responded, 'Here am I, send me.' (Isaiah 6, vs. 2–8)

God sent him with a message, and Isaiah went on a mission to serve the Lord.

The seraphim had probably lost their serpent form and appeared in human shape, or perhaps part-human and part-animal. Their duty was to praise God, and probably to guard the entrance to His presence, of which smoke was a symbol. The prophecy was of complete destruction, symbolising the righteous remnant which contained the promise of the future (the Messiah).

Paul had his famous vision on the road to Damascus, in which he was transformed. He underwent a transformation in person-hood which was a turning-point from darkness, chaos, and void into light. Paul was a persecutor. At the time he was on his way to kill those who had given themselves to Jesus. Thus 'a light from heaven flashed unto Paul. He fell down to the ground and heard a voice saying: 'Saul, Saul, why do you persecute me?' Paul asked, 'Who are you?' The Lord said, 'I am Jesus, whom you are persecut-ing, but rise and enter the city and you will be told what you are to do.' (Acts 9, vs. 3–6, RSV)

Through this Vision Paul changed dramatically, showing again the power of visions. visions, I could say, play a very important role in the lives of men, just as dreams do. Paul was a very learned man. He met some preachers, before this vision incident, who talked about Jesus. But Paul did not listen. He consented to Stephen's death and persecuted Christians for what they preached. In other words, he persecuted those who spoke about Jesus. But through a vision he changed dramatically and became a leader among the apostles.

Again, a vision made Paul go to Macedonia. While there, many people gave themselves to Christ. Presumably Christianity would have been different if Paul had not listened to his vision.

Paul had another vision while at sea. They were threatened by the sea and thought they were going to die. The prisoners thought they were going to be killed by the soldiers. But an angel appeared to Paul in a vision and assured him they were safe. Paul passed the message to everyone in the boat. Paul's vision strengthened everyone's hearts. From this I deduce that the effect of visions can encourage, strengthen and give hope.

God speaks to us in different ways: sometimes through visions, sometimes directly, as Jesus did to the other apostles. Thus, while some people have doubted the whole question of dream, in my view dreams change the hearts of people and make them better people. Paul was transformed and started a new life. He became his true self. Jung, quoted by Ullman *et al.*, explains that in such dreams the self is the central archetype, often appearing in images of wholeness or completeness. This is so because the self is the totality of the human personality.

Indeed, denying dream power is to deny the Bible as well. Thus, dreams would cease to exist if they were from men and would continue to exist if they were from God, and are a means by which God reveals himself to people every day.

Dreams: a motivation to religious action

Martin Luther King's famous speech shows that a dream can be possible. He had a dream in 1963 about black people's liberation in the USA. Whether his dream might have been a rhetorical statement or described an actual dream, it is certainly a great vision of what can be possible: Thus he stated; 'I have a dream, that one day the sons of former slaves and the sons of former slave-owners will be able to sit down together at the table of brotherhood. That my four children will one day live in a nation where they will not be judged by the colour of their skin but by the content of their character. One day little black boys and black girls will be able to join hands with little white boys and white girls and walk together as sisters and brothers. Jews and Gentiles, Protestants and Catholics, will be able to join hands and sing in the words of that old Negro spiritual, 'Free at last'.

Martin Luther King's use of the present tense, 'have', as opposed to the past, 'had', would seem to suggest that his dream is a Utopian vision rather than an actual remembered dream. Bearing in mind the period when he delivered this powerful speech, one would be tempted to regard his 'dream' as a moral challenge to 'the American dream,' the nature of which is essentially materialistic.

It could perhaps be argued that King's 'dream' has become more realisable now. There have been a number of critical reforms, i.e. anti-discrimination laws, the right to vote, etc. But is any idea or vision ever absolutely impossible?

The position of the black population in American has certain parallels with the position of women, i.e. although a legal frame-work has been implemented against racism/sexism, on a covert psychological level much of the prejudice still remains in the USA.

Equally, some people felt sufficiently threatened by Martin Luther's 'dream' to oppose the ideals in it even more vigorously than before. However, whether it was the actual dream or some sort of visualisation, our interest is that what he stated became possible. Some people can imagine the future and that imagination is like a dream.

Great religions dreams and their universality

Dreams have also played a great role in the foundation of other religions.

Dreams have such considerable influence in the faith of religious believers that they accept them as divine revelation. The Old Testament dreams are viewed in the context of manifestation of prophetic testimonies. Each of the fifteen dreams reported in the Old Testament signifies an historical accomplishment of an event. For example, the dream of Joseph which brought Israel out of Egypt, or the dream of Daniel which protected the chosen people of God from contamination by Babylon. The Israelites were an oppressed people who used dreams as a propaganda weapon of power. They believed in a universal monarch on their side who will help them conquer and dominate the whole world.

There is, however, a similarity in the dreams of World religions. This is confirmed by Raymond de Becker when he states; 'The role of dreams in the Judaeo-Christian tradition was apparently similar to that in Buddhism and Islam. The vocations of both Jesus, the Buddha and Muhammad were foretold in dreams.[15] To this end a linkage between Judaeo-Christian tradition and other religions could be drawn. At the beginning of this chapter, I stated that most ancient societies regarded dreams as a channel of com-munication between this world and the 'other world'. This applies to the universality of dreams as well in any great system of religion/belief in an 'other world'.

Buddhism

The vocation of Buddha was announced and defined by a series of dreams. This was also similar to the vocation of Jesus, as has already been pointed out.

Maya, the blessed mother of Buddha, was to conceive and give birth to a universal monarch who would lead the simple life of a monk and abandon all the desires of life. According to tradition, it was predicted that he would be a great universal teacher, and that four signs would show him which vocation he would follow. His father apparently made an effort to prevent him from going outside the palace.

His birth was a miraculous one and was attended by many strange portents. He was seen in the legends as one who in previous births had been prepared for a special task in this life. H. Saddhatissa (1976) tells us that 'after Buddha's birth a venerable sage named Kala Devela offered his respects to the new prince, and told king Saddhadanon that his son was to be a man out of the ordinary.'[16] The dream came true. His father wanted him to be a prince but the Buddha chose the other direction. He experienced something under the Bu tree and gathered his disciples. Here we see how strong a dream is. The father tried to persuade him to be a prince, but he failed. Despite such difficult circumstances, the Buddha became the founder of the Buddhist religion.

Islam

Dream activity was also basic to the vocation of Muhammad, the founder of the Islamic faith. Muhammad received his mission in a vision which lasted six months. His revelations were communicated to him by God and during this period the Koran, the holy book of Islam, was alleged to have come down from heaven in its entirety. Idowu, in his book *African Traditional Religion*, gives an implied warning in a story told about Muhammad's visit to Allah for the purpose of receiving the scheme for the daily obligatory prayer. It is said that when Muhammad arrived at the outer court of heaven, he saw a voluminous garment, the ends of which, height or breadth, he could not see because of its infinite size. It was Allah's garment. It is said that he was confronted with a bewildering sight when he arrived in the presence of Allah. He saw Allah but could not describe the sight. The angels, seeing the bewilderment of Muhammad, sang out: 'We eagerly expect to see what form of salutation Muhammad will use for the Lord . . .'[17]

Indeed, Muhammad had a great respect for dreams. It is believed that much of the Koran was dictated to him in a dream. In this sense the Koran came from heaven, as had been pointed out before. Muhammad used to ask his disciples each morning of what they had dreamed, then interpreted those dreams which appeared to strengthen the faith. Just as in Judaic dream theory, there is in Islam a distinction between divine and false dreams. Interpreters, as Montague Ullman *et al*. put in their book *Working with Dreams*, are necessary and false prophets warned against.[18]

I have shown in this chapter that there is no difference between religions, even though Buddhism claims there is no 'God', unlike Islam, Christianity and Judaism. There is also no difference between Old and New Testament dreams/visions. Thus it would seem that dreams are neutral and their source cannot be identified as of the Christian God. Whether He exists or not is a different matter. But the most important thing is truth. If that's the case we might become heretics; hence one could say that there are many expressions of truth, all valid in God's eyes.

This chapter has discussed biblical dreams as they are narrated in the Bible. Dreams and visions of both the Old Testament and the New are discussed. It has been shown that the prophets in Judaeo-Christianity took dreams seriously and trusted and believed in a dream, as we have seen in the case of Gideon when he went to fight with the Midianites. Joseph was made a great man through dream interpretation. As with Christianity in the New Testament, Joseph listened to what the Lord told him through his dream and decided to take Mary as his wife. A linkage has been shown between Judaeo-Christianity, Budhhism and Islam.

Chapter 7

Dream as a Problem-Solver

I am of the opinion that there are guardian spirits. Be they angelic or not, these guardian spirits exist to help us solve our problems. Unlike the popular view that spirits emerge only during sleep, I will be arguing here that spirits also appear and communicate with people during daytime. They act through telepathy. What makes a person from the 'other side' communicate with us is nothing but these guardian spirits.

This chapter examines the question of dream as a problem-solver. Dream as a problem-solver is a recent theory which was started and popularised fifty years ago in the West. Evidence, however, seems to indicate that the role of dreams in problem-solving existed much earlier than this in Australia, among the Aborigines, and in Africa.

The Australian Aborigines migrated from south-east Asia about 30,000 years ago. They were originally semi-nomadic people who lived by hunting and gathering, but have today been assimilated into Western élite cultures. Aboriginal mythology was generally rich and elaborate and included accounts of creation during the primordial dawn, which they call 'dream time'.[1] The principal issues in Aboriginal social life were religious and economic, including ownership of land, which was non-transferable. Its members held land in trust collectively by means of an unwritten charter deriving from dream.[2] On the religious side 'life and death were not seen as being diametrically opposed. The dream provided a thread of life, even in physical death.'[3]

In Africa dream as a problem-solver also existed ages ago. Our grandparents solved their problems by listening to dreams, as has already been made clear in Chapter 3.

Moreover, there is written evidence from English literature to indicate that the role of dream in problem-solving was recognised in Western cultures. For instance, John Abercrombie, physician to Queen Victoria in Scotland, demonstrated that there were mental operations in dreams of a more intellectual character than was generally appreciated. He cited a testimonial from a colleague, who claimed that thoughts which he had in dreams were so good in their reasoning, illustration and language that he used them in his college lectures and in his written works.[4]

A very good example is that of the Marquis de Condoret, a brilliant mathematician before becoming a philosopher. Brian Inglis wrote about Condoret: 'When engaged in some profound and obscure calculations, he was often obliged to leave them in an incomplete state, and retire to bed to rest; and that the remaining steps, and the conclusion of his calculations, had more than once revealed themselves in his dreams.'[5]

Another good example is that of a great friend of mine. Not only she but also her family are close to my own. Her name is Mrs Margaret Chikhadzula. She came over to Britain to do a Master's degree in accountancy at Glasgow University.

She had a dream in her final year, in June 1989. She was anxious to hear her exam results so that she could complete her dissertation and go back to Malawi. Although she was studying, her mind was on her children. She was scared of the possibility of failing her exams, since it would mean extending her stay in Britain.

She did not want to stay on the university campus after the exams; she wanted to forget. She went to stay with an English family. In her dream she dreamt that I had sent an apple. The apple had the word congratulations written all over it.

With this dream she knew she had passed her exams. She then decided to go back to the campus to start working on her dissertation. After two weeks the results came out and she had passed in all subjects.

Brian Inglis gives the example of Colin Forrest who was at the time anxious to qualify as a nurse and was working to pass his next examination. In a dream he saw his dead father (a naval surgeon), looking about twenty-five years old, in a brilliant white gown, and the father said, 'The thyroid gland.' Colin's first nursing exam was next day at the Royal West Sussex Hospital, Chichester, and he was so struck with the dream that he looked up the thyroid that morning, and it was there in the exam, so he answered it well.'[6]

A friend of mine knows of a vision of a man who never had any problem completing his exams, for in each case the paper came to him in a dream, enabling him to prepare for the exam with total confidence – and, not surprisingly, excellent results!

A workmate by the name of Sue McGuire, a Development Officer for Social Services in Liverpool, told me that she found dreams extremely helpful in her essay writing while she was at Birmingham University. Each time, a dream came to her the night before she had to write an essay. She could write it on a piece of paper the way it ought to be written. In the morning she could write it again very nicely and then write the essay exactly how it appeared in the dream. She had confidence she was going to get high marks because the dream helped her to write the essay.

Lost property

Other most vivid dreams are those of lost property. Andrew Lang, historian, folklore expert and classicist, noted in his book of dreams (*Ghost*, 1897) that dreams can provide information which subsequently turns out to be correct, of a kind which the dreamer did not know that he knew, and was very anxious to know. He cited the case of a barrister of his acquaintance who sat up late one night to write letters and after midnight went out to post them.

He missed a cheque for a large sum on undressing. He looked for it everywhere but could not find it. He later dreamt the cheque curled round an area railing not far from his own door. He got up and walked down the street, and found it.[7]

This also occurred to me while I was in Malawi in 1956. I lost a ten-shilling note. I searched everywhere, but I could not find it. I gave up and decided not to worry about it. One night I dreamt the ten-shilling note was between some dried leaves in the yard outside our house, camouflaged among the dried leaves, making it therefore difficult to see. The dream told me exactly where it was lying. I had this dream round about 3.00 a.m. When I woke up I did not go to sleep but waited for daybreak so that I could go and pick it up. In the morning I went outside and my sister asked me where I was going. I told her I was going to look for my ten shillings. She asked me, 'Do you think the ten-shilling note is still there waiting for you, can't other people pick it up?' I told her it was there. I went quickly and found it just as the dream had told me. I showed it to my sister and she was surprised.

On day-to-day problems

Brian Inglis wrote in the *Guardian*, 9 September 1987, that perhaps the commonest and certainly the most welcome of useful dreams is the problem-solver. Many people apparently follow the example of Sir Walter Scott, who, when at a loss for the solution to something which baffled him, would tell himself confidently, 'Never mind, we shall have it at seven o'clock tomorrow morning.'[8] Evidently sleeping on it helped. Even when I was very young, I still knew what was going on in my family. It happened that the family had no money to buy anything, e.g. soap, food, etc., to the extent that on Saturdays they could not go to the market. But going to the market was a tradition to some people: even if they had only ten pence they would still go. My sister Anandau was one such person.

My family were, however, worried during the previous night; they had no money to buy vegetables, meat, tomatoes, etc. They left the problem as it was: 'Sleeping on it,' as Sir Walter Scott might have put it, or Henry Reed, in the chapter 'Dream Pillow' from his book, *Getting Help from your Dreams*. I had a dream. My family were worried about what to eat the following day. I dreamt I was at the market and found a ten-shilling note. In the morning my sister went to the market. She did not have any money, but she just wanted to buy vegetables and tomatoes, which would have cost her twenty pence or less. I followed her. She refused me and she kept on stopping to make sure I was not coming. I stopped if I saw she was watching me and started running again when I could see she was not looking back. By the time she reached the market, so too had I. She kept quiet; she could not do anything, because I was there.

Realising I'd not be sent back any more, I kept her company and helped her with the shopping. I was going around the stalls when I found a ten-shilling note lying on the ground. I picked it and gave it to my sister. She wondered where I got it; I told her. She asked her friends whether some one had lost it. Everyone said 'no' and they said it was probably the group which was there before. They suggested to my sister that she gave it to me to buy things I wanted, such as sugar cane, bananas, etc. They all said it was my good luck the spirits had given it to me. My sister told them she could not give it to me: 'We have nothing, absolutely nothing, in the house.' At that time ten shillings was a lot of money. With it my sister managed to buy even meat.

After the market I walked home with Anandau, carrying lots and lots of foodstuffs and some sugar cane, of which I was very fond as a child. Everyone at the house wondered where we got the money to buy all those things. My sister told them, 'Mary found the money at the market.' Someone said to her, but you told her not to come. My sister laughed: She just knew someone was going to mention that.

My interpretation is different, though, from Henry Reed's. As he has indicated, 'sleeping on it' to some meant putting something under your pillow in order to dream that thing. In his dream realisations, Henry Reed included instructions on writing a 'pillow letter' to your dreams asking for help on the specific problem of concern, and then putting that letter under the pillow to literally, sleep on it. Henry Reed states, 'In the feedback reports from the hundreds of people who have tested this work book, again there was an indication that many people followed the instruction, in spite of their doubts about it, and found that it produced a dream. It often does seem to work, but how or why it works remains unclear.'[9]

'Sleeping on it,' in my own interpretation, means sleeping while thinking about a particular problem and in the end one dreams of the same thing. It is like dream coming within someone's mind. Equally it is difficult to pass a value judgment. I remember some of my colleagues when I was at a secondary school used to sleep with a letter from their boyfriends under their pillows and in the morning they could share their dream experiences with us. This also agrees with Henry Reed.

Guardian spirits

In 1989 I had some problems at work and decided to leave my
job. I kept telling myself happiness was more important than
money. As I was contemplating resigning, I had a dream on 27
June that year. The scene was like a college and the buildings
were halls of residence. I had my own room with a communal
cooking area. My niece, Joyce Thadzi, came to the kitchen with
food, which she had just bought. She was with two girls, Hannah
Mabasa (Mrs Kawalewale), an old schoolfriend, and Nellie Sakah,
who is now married and lives in Canada; she too had been my
schoolmate. None of them spoke to me. Eventually they all
vanished.

There were also many other people on the play. Everyone was
doing their own thing. There were two black girls and many white
girls. I tried to be friendly to these two black girls, but each time
I spoke to them they would vanish. However, in the end we all
went in the dining hall, which was full of people eating. All of a
sudden one English girl came up to me, saying my father wanted
me outside. I went down to meet him. He put on a red coat and
a red hat. The coat was brighter than normal and it looked very
expensive. It had big black buttons. Under the coat he wore an
African robe. He was wearing old slippers and carrying a walking
stick.

I grabbed him and cried, 'Oh, my father, come and walk with
me.' I held him by the hand. I invited him for a cup of tea. My
father was fond of tea before he died. He walked quickly when
he heard me mentioning a cup of tea. But he asked a question:
'Do they really allow non-residents to go in the dining room?' I
replied, 'Yes, they do.' So we went towards the dining room. As
we started climbing the steps, my father said. 'What is this thing
that makes you think of leaving your job? Leaving the job when
people are suffering at home? No, don't leave the job, my daughter. Besides, you don't quit jobs when you are at odds with your
workmates. It is better to leave in peace.' No sooner had he
finished his last sentence then he disappeared and I found myself
all alone.

I woke up and started looking around my room to see whether
he was sitting somewhere. But to my disappointment there was
no trace of him. However, I realised later it was only a dream. I

took a pen and my diary and recorded the dream, and drew his picture at the same time. With this type of dream I came to the conclusion that surely there must be some guardian spirits somewhere. They see us when we are perplexed and come to strengthen us.

In response to the advice from my father, who died ages ago, I went to my place of work and started afresh. Dream is indeed useful. It helps us during times of indecision.

Dreaming of being anaemic

In 1986 I dreamt I was anaemic; the word was actually written. At the same time there was a sore on my right leg. I got up and checked my leg to see whether there was a lump, but there was nothing and I felt relieved. I kept the dream to myself, more especially as the lump I had dreamt of was not there on my leg.

The afternoon of that same day a lump actually did appear on my leg. First I felt like scratching. I touched the place, just to confirm that the lump was actually there; since the dream had already told me, I just started eating the right diet. But more sores appeared on my leg. I then decided to go to my GP and he told me I was a bit anaemic. He instructed me to eat a lot of fruits, particularly oranges, and lots of tomatoes, lettuce, cucumber, etc. He also mentioned that I needed iron food. I wrote to Sister Alma Binder in the USA. She is a nurse and she supported me when I was doing my Master's degree. She told me to use Marmite on my bread. The dream sort of frightened me. I thought it might be something serious to reach to that extent of dreaming.

Edgar Cayce, in his book, *The World's Greatest Psychic*, interprets dreams by Frances, who was dreaming about her health problems. Frances had put herself on a diet; she cut out starches and sweets. One night, she told me, 'I dreamt I said to my husband, "Now my cramps are all gone." Then I awakened and all the pain was gone.'[10] Cayce interpreted the dream to mean that the cramps were caused by her reducing diet.

After a week, however, Frances had another dream. This time, she dreamt she was eating lots and lots of chocolate, cakes and all kinds of sweets.

Cayce explained to her again that it was a 'problem-solving

dream for her body, and that she should eat more sweets, rather than damaging her body by a reducing diet'.[11]

One of my workmates in the Administration Department, Anne Johnston, aged twenty, was amazed at how dreams can help to solve problems in real-life situations. She writes: 'I never really cried when my grandmother died, although having had a close relationship with her I was extremely upset. The main reason for not shedding tears was my mum. I felt that if she saw me in a state, it would make her worse than she was already. I began to have nightmares that really troubled my night's sleep. I told my mum and my aunt of these dreams, and they thought that it could be the result of anxiety. The nightmares continued over a period of weeks. Then one night I dreamt my family and myself were seated in the dining room of my house. Everything was perfectly normal, when my grandmother appeared. In the dream she was a ghost. She began to tell us that everything was fine, that she was free from pain, how she loved us all and how she would be looking after us. Then she disappeared. After this dream I never suffered another nightmare.' As we see from this story, there are many of us who have been helped by dream to stop worrying; only some people are, alas, not prepared to accept this. They regard dreams as irrational. I always tend to wonder why dreams are regarded as irrational when they have helped people in real-life situations. The girl above would not have stopped having nightmares if she had not heeded her dreams.

Another good example is that of Elias Howe. He had been trying fruitlessly to work out how a lockstitch sewing-machine could be made. He had this dream in 1844. 'Cold sweat poured down his brow, his hands shook with fear, his knees quaked. Try as he would, the inventor could not get the missing figure in the problem over which he had worked so long. All this was so real to him that he cried aloud. In the vision he saw himself surrounded by dark-skinned and painted warriors, who formed a hollow square about him and led him to a place of execution. Suddenly he noticed that near the heads of the spears which his guards carried, there were eye-shaped holes! He had solved the secret! What he needed was a needle with an eye near the point! He awoke from his dream, sprang out of bed, and at once made a whittled model of an eye-pointed needle, with which he brought his experiments to a successful close.'[12] From this dream we can see that our extra sixth sense can be more revealing than any other. Without it, some things would never have been discovered.

Dream telepathy

Dream telepathy is related to problem-solving.

The *Concise Oxford Dictionary* defines telepathy as the communication between people of thoughts, feelings, etc., involving mechanisms that cannot be understood in terms of known scientific laws.

Dreams have also been regarded by some as a means of communication: getting messages from people who are far from us. This was not plausible in my eyes until recently. Just as I was about to finish my book I had a vivid dream about my brother. He has never phoned me since he left Britain.

On 15 February 1991, at 7.46 a.m., I had a dream in which my brother, Stensfield Chinkwita, was sharing his problems with me. My brother used to live in London. He was telling me of his problems, the contents of which will I cannot reveal. While he was in the middle of telling me all these problems a telephone rang. I normally dream in the morning and this time it was 7.46 a.m., as already mentioned. I went to answer the phone to find that it was my brother. He started telling me problems of a different kind, as had already been stated. What I had been dreaming was what he told me on the phone. I was amazed and did not know how on earth this could have happened.

A dream is thought to come from an outside agency, as R. Cartwright has stated in his book *Night Life*. As with dream telepathy, it is believed our minds are more open to thought messages from others than they are ordinarily (Krippner, Ullman and Vaughn, 1973).[13] R. Cartwright then suggests that perhaps dreaming is a state in which we can be influenced by others without our awareness, rather like hypnosis.[14] Not that someone had made you sleep, as we have explained about dreams taken in the lab in Chapter 1. But there must be a reason for one to sleep. That a dream has been the means by which someone who has communicated his thoughts to the other person's mind.

I was fascinated to read of a dream of a similar kind. Brenda Mallon, in her book *Women Dreaming*, says that she had a dream in which her two cousins were present. When she woke up she was miserable and sad all day. After three weeks she had a telephone call which informed her that her sister, Rona, was in intensive care. She had had a brain haemorrhage and her condition was critical. Brenda flew to West Germany to see her. Upon her arrival she learned that at the time she had had the dream her sister had suffered a minor clot in the brain which her doctors had not been able to diagnose.[15]

At the beginning of this chapter, I argued that these guardian angels come to us even during the day. For example, I have a friend, Brian Ragbourn, who used to live in Liverpool and later moved to London. He never telephoned me after he left Liverpool. Then I was supposed to attend a course in London but I forgot about it. I assumed that 'Personnel' had booked everything. A telephone call came from the course organiser in London to ask me whether I was still going to attend the course, since they had heard nothing from me. The course was the following day. My line manager, Phil Purvis, told me not to go since we had not booked the hotel. He said, 'We must not hear that you slept in the streets.' I told him God was going to provide. I was not going to sleep in the streets, but I stood by the original plan.

I hoped I was going to sleep at a friend's place, Sarah, from Sudan. I did not have her telephone number. My friend Grace Jalwang kept on giving me her telephone number and I kept on losing it. This day I phoned Grace to ask for Sarah's phone number, only to hear Sarah had left that same day for Nigeria to see her husband, who was working there.

I did not know what to do. I decided to go to London and ask the people who organised the course to help me book the hotel. In the end I thought of ringing Professor Peters, who is a father to one of the families which was keeping Brian in London. I rang Professor Peters to ask if he could give me the family's number; unfortunately he was not in. Apparently he had travelled somewhere. I was then stranded, not knowing what to do. I said to myself, 'Let me go to bed, tomorrow will bring its own problems.' As I was going to bed, the telephone went; it was around 10.00 p.m. It was Brian.

I said to myself this is not just a coincidence, there must be something beyond that. There must be guardian angels. I don't know whether this could be categorised as telepathy or synchronicity, as Carl Jung puts it. It follows, then, that these angelic guardian angels do take care of us even during the day, when we are awake! R. de Becker supports this in his book *The Understanding of Dreams' or 'The Machinations of the Night*, in which he states, 'The existence of so-called telepathic phenomena is in principle quite possible, since they can also be studied as products of the waking state.'[16] Dream telepathy existed ages ago and probably in every generation there had been some people who have experienced it. Becker also states that, in the last century, metaphysical societies collected many documents witnessing 'telepathic' occurrences in the waking and dream states. These documents were in favour of the theory, but it was impossible to reproduce it experimentally. Experiments were, however, made by different researchers and Charles Richet proved that hypnosis and telepathy were not necessarily connected, using mathematics of chance to evaluate the results.[17]

In 1921, Freud wrote an essay on psychoanalysis and telepathy in which he claimed that 'it no longer seemed possible to neglect the study of so-called occult facts'. For this reason he reported three cases in which he was strongly convinced that clairvoyants had seen, by the transmission of thought, what their consultors had more or less consciously wanted. They had facts of both the past and the present. Freud's essay on dreams and telepathy[17] reported the case of one of his correspondents who dreamt of his second wife giving birth to twins. Subsequently his second wife's daughter gave birth to twins.

As I now see it, dream as a whole is very useful; more importantly, many a dream can be a problem-solver. I have, in most cases, been helped in solving my problems through dreams! The time I had some problems at work the whole of that week I had wished I could meet Rachel Alonge, a friend of mine who works as a secretary with the Liverpool Social Services, District 'D'. I knew her through her husband, Charles Alogne, who was doing a Doctorate degree in Town Planning, with Liverpool University. I was at the time doing my MA degree with the same University. Rachel and Charles are very devoted Christians and do help a lot in time of difficulty. A lot of overseas students go to Rachel and Charles for help. At this particular time I wished I could meet her or Grace Jal-wang to see what they had to say about my problems. By then Rachel had started working and there was no one at the house. Charles also had just moved to London where he had obtained a job in Planning. Grace, on the other hand, was always out. Each time I rang there was no reply. As a consequence I developed a terrible headache, because I was failing to make a decision. But in the end I had my father's dream in which he advised me not to leave work. He only wanted me to leave when in harmony with everyone at work.

I am also strongly convinced that dream telepathy is not implausible. Some sorts of mechanism do happen in our brain to the extent that messages are transmitted to us through dreams. My brother had a problem and that problem had already been communicated to me in a dream before he actually spoke to me. I was then more able to understand him, since a dream had already told me. With all this in mind I cannot hesitate to say that we surely have guardian angels. They take care of us, awake or asleep. This vindicates the argument that dreams descend from God, to protect us or to take care of us. In this sense dream is truly very useful.

Conclusion

Dream has played a dominant role in the lives of mankind since history began. It means so much to so many people. It brings happiness and sadness as well as inspiration and despondency.

Some people see it as a revelation of important events in their past, present and future lives. Some see it as a sign of good fortune. Others see it as a bad omen.

The old prophets and heroes of the biblical era used it as a powerful medium of communication with God. It found expression in their visions and prophecies.

The concept of dream is so enigmatic that even scientific investigations have not succeeded in fully unravelling it. It is generally interlaced with our spiritual and emotional feelings and finds expression in the semiconscious state of our minds.

Sometimes the fulfilment of life's ambition is only achieved in the dream. At other times, it provides the inspiration to achieve such ambitions.

The painful feeling of the loss of a loved one in a dream is a measure of how deeply one cares and gives an insight into one's emotional response if such a loss occurs in real life.

Although dream is an integral part of our everyday life, there is no answer to the question of why we dream and how dreams occur.

The answer remains as enigmatic as the history of creativity, the history of the universe, and associated big bang and dark hole – and how we came to be on this earth.

References

Chapter 1

1. Sutherland, S., 'Mixing Memory and Desire', book review in *TLS*, 22 November 1985, p. 1319.
2. Blackmore, S., 'Dreams That Do What They're Told' *New Scientist*, 6 January 1990.
3. Hearne, K. M. T. 'Control your Own Dream' *New Scientist*, 24 September 1981.
4. *Ibid*.
5. Blackmore, S., *Sunday Times*, 3 June 1990.
6. Blacmore, S., 'Dream That Do What They're Told', *New Scientist*, 6 January 1990.
7. *Ibid*.
8. Blackmore, S., *Sunday Times*, 3 June 1990.
9. Blackmore, S., 'Dreams That Do What They're Told', *New Scientist*, 6 January 1990.
10. Hearne, K. M. T. *Lucid Dreams*. Thesis submitted to Liverpool University, 1978, p. 97.
11. De Becker, R. *The Understanding of Dreams*, George Allen & Unwin, London, 1968, p. 251.
12. *Ibid*., p. 252.
13. *Ibid*.
14. *Ibid*.
15. *Ibid*.
16. Cartwright, R., *Night Life*, Prentice Hall International, New Jersey, 1977, p. 20.
17. Green, L. 1963, quoted by Hearne, K., in *Lucid Dreams*, thesis submitted to Liverpool University, 1978, p. 102.
18. Malcolm, N. *Dreaming*, Routledge & Kegan Paul, New York, 1959, pp. 72–3.
19. Jouvet, M., 'The States of Sleep', *Scientific American*, 1967, p. 66.
20. *Ibid*.
21. Kleitman, N., 'Patterns of Dreaming', *Scientific American*, November 1960, p. 82.
22. *Ibid*.

23. Blackmore, S., 'Dreams That Do What They're Told', *New Scientist*, 6 January 1990, p. 49.
24. Dee, N., *Your Dreams and What They Mean*, Aquarian Press, UK, 1984, p. 42.
25. Kleitman, N., *op. cit.*, p. 85.
26. Blackmore, S., *op. cit.*, p. 49.
27. *Ibid.*
28. Dee, N., *op. cit.*, p. 41.
29. Parker, R., *Healing Dreams*, SPCK, London, 1988, p. 17.
30. *Ibid.*
31. *Ibid.*
32. Freud, S., *The Interpretation of Dreams*, Penguin Books, 1975, p. 199.
33. Faraday, A., *Dream Power*, Pan Books, London, 1972, p. 52.
34. *Ibid.*, pp. 52–53.
35. *Ibid.*, p. 53.
36. Dee, N., *op. cit.*, p. 58.
37. Parker, R., *Healing Dreams*, SPCK, London, 1988, p. 18.
38. Hearne, H. K. T., *Lucid Dreams*, thesis submitted to Liverpool University, 1978, p. 72.
39. Jung, C. G., *Memories, Dreams, Reflection*, Collins/Routledge & Kegan Paul, London, 1973, p. 333.
40. Parker, R., *op. cit.*, p. 19.
41. Dee, N., *op. cit.*, p. 61.
42. Ullman, M., *et al.*, *Working with Dreams*, Aquarian Press, Los Angeles, 1987, p. 60.
43. Mackenzie, N., *Dreams and Dreaming*, Aldus Books, London, 1965, p. 53.
44. Cartwright, R. D., *Night Life*, Prentice-Hall International, New Jersey, 1977, p. 120.
45. *Ibid.*, P. 120.
46. Dee, N., *op. cit.*, p. 63.
47. *Ibid.*
48. Gwinn, R. P., *et al.*, *The New Encyclopaedia Britannica*, Vol. 10 ('Micropaedia'), Chicago, 15th edn (1974–90), p. 638.
49. Holman, D., *The Green Torture*, Robert Hale, London, 1962, p. 92.
50. *Ibid.*, p. 92.
51. *Ibid.*, p. 93.
52. *Ibid.*, p. 94.
53. *Ibid.*, p. 95.
54. *Ibid.*, p. 98.
55. *Ibid.*, p. 99.
56. Ferguson, Jane, in the *Guardian*, 26 April 1989, p. 27.
57. Ranger *et al.*, *The Historical Study of African Religion*, Heinemann, London, 1972, p. 11.
58. Sutherland, S., 'Mixing Memory and Desire', review in *TLS*, 22 November 1985.

Chapter 2

1. Jung, C. G., *Memories, Dreams and Reflection*, Pentheon Books, New York, 1963, pp. 285–6.
2. Parker, R., *Healing Dreams*, SPCK, London, 1988, p. 23.
3. Dudley, G. A., *Dreams: Their Mysteries Revealed*, Aquarian Press, UK, 1969, p. 73.
4. Medawar, P., in S. Sutherland, 'Mixing Memory and Desire', *TLS*, 22 November 1985.
5. Jung, C. G., *Ibid*.
6. Reed, H., *Getting Help From Your Dreams*, Inner Vision Publishing Company, Virginia Beach, 1985, p. 39.
7. Crick, F., in Sutherland, *op. cit.*
8. Jung, C. G., *Memories, Dreams and Reflections*, Collins, Routledge & Kegan Paul, London, 1973, p. 288.
9. *Ibid.*, p. 289.
10. Faraday, A., *op. cit.*, p. 56.
11. Dudley, G. A., *op. cit.*, p. 70.
12. Gustavus Hindman Miller, *The Dictionary of Dreams*, Blacketon-Hall, UK, 1983, p. 597.
13. *Ibid.*, p. 518.
14. Ullman, M., *et al.*, *Working With Dreams*, Aquarian Press, Los Angeles, USA, 1987, p. 81.

Chapter 3

1. Mbiti, J. S., *African Religion And Philosophy*, Heinemann, London, 1969, p. 1.
2. *Ibid.*
3. Parrinder, E. G. P., *African Traditional Religion*, Sheldon Press, London (Third Edition 1974), p. 40.
4. Idowu, B. E., *African Traditional Religion*, SCM Press, London, 1973, p. 140.
5. Ranger and Kimambo, *The Historical Study Of African Religion*, Heinemann, London, 1972, p. 174.
6. *Ibid.*, p. 40.
7. *Ibid.*, p. 175.
8. *Ibid.*, p. 176.
9. Whisson, M. G., *et al.*, *Religious and Social Change in Southern Africa: Anthropological Essays*, David Philip, Cape Town, 1975, p. 18.
10. Ranger, *et al.*, *op. cit.*, p. 97.
11. Stent, D., *Religious Studies Made Simple*, Heinemann, London, 1983, p. 6.
12. *Ibid.*
13. Rowie, R. H., *Primitive Religion*, Peter Owen Ltd, London, 1960, p. 8.

14. Simpson, G. E., *Religious Cults of the Caribbean*, University of Puerto Rico, 1970, p. 122.
15. Callaway, Revd. C., *The Religious System of the Amazulu*, Trubner & Co., London, 1970, p. 232.
16. *Ibid*.
17. Taylor, J. V., *The Primal Vision*, SCM Press Ltd, London, 1973, p. 149.
18. *Ibid.*, p. 151.
19. Idowu, B. E., *African Traditional Religion*, SCM Press Ltd, London, 1973, p. 176.
20. Callaway, C., *op. cit.*, p. 228.
21. Sundkler, B., *Christian Ministry in Africa*, SCM Press, London, 1960, p. 26.
22. *Ibid.*, p. 20.
23. *Ibid.*, p. 42.

Chapter 4

1. John 3. v. 3.
2. Romans 6. v. 3 RSV.
3. Romans 6. vs. 5, 6, 8 & 9.
4. Peak, A. S., *Peak's Commentary on the Bible*, Thomas Nelson & Sons, London, 1919, p. 822.
5. *Collins Concise English Dictionary*.
6. *Collier's Encyclopaedia*, Vol. 22, New York, (1970), p. 416.
7. Gwinn, R. P. *et al. The New Encyclopaedia Britannica*, Vol. 10 ('Micropaedia'), Chicago, 15th edn (1974–90), p. 25.
8. *Ibid*.
9. Stevenson, L., *Seven Theories of Human Nature*, Oxford University Press, 1974, p. 26.
10. Gwinn, R. P. *et al., op. cit.*
11. Murray, D. C., *Reincarnation Ancient: Beliefs and Modern Evidence*, David & Charles, Newton Abbot, 1981, p. 17.
12. *Ibid.*, p. 29.
13. *Ibid*.
14. Jung, C. G., *Memories, Dreams, Reflections*, Pantheon Books, New York, 1961, pp. 291, 318.
15. *Ibid.*, pp. 319, 322.
16. Murray, D. C., *op. cit.*, p. 35.
17. Murray, D. C., *op. cit.*, p. 126.
18. Cranston, S., *et al.*, *Reincarnation: A New Horizon in Science, Religion And Society*, Julian Press, New York, 1984, p. 82.

Chapter 5

1. Dee, N., *Your Dreams and What They Mean*, Aquarian Press, UK, 1984, p. 31.
2. Inglis, B., *Guardian*, September 1987.
3. Fornari, A., 'Understanding Dream Psychology' in *How To Interpret Dreams*, Hamlyn, London, 1989, p. 9.
4. Dee, N., *op. cit.*, p. 13–14.
5. Dee, N., *op. cit.*, p. 14.
6. Dee, N., *op. cit.*, p. 15.
7. Dee, N., *op. cit.*, p. 16.
8. Kelsey, M., *Dreams a Way To Listen To God*, Paulist Press, New York, 1978, p. 71.
9. *Ibid*.
10. Inglis, B., *The Power of Dreams*, Paladin/Grafton Books, London, 1988, p. 194.
11. Ullman, M. *et al.*, *Working with Dreams*, Aquarian Press, New York, 1987, p. 40.
12. Miller, G. H., *The Dictionary of Dreams*, Blaketon-Hall, Devon, 1983, p. 8.
13. De Becker, R., *The Understanding of Dreams*, George Allen & Unwin, London, 1968, pp. 193–8.
14. MacKenzie, N., *Dreams and Dreaming*, Aldus Books, London, 1965, p. 58.
15. Dee, N., *op. cit.*, p. 25.
16. Kelsey, M., *op. cit.*, p. 72.
17. Kelsey, M., *op. cit.*, p. 73.
18. Kelsey, M., *op. cit.*, p. 73.
19. Dee, N., *op. cit.*, p. 24.
20. Ullman, M., *op. cit.*, p. 43.
21. Ullman, M., *op. cit.*, p. 43.
22. Kelsey, M., *op. cit.*, p. 74.
23. Dee, N., *op. cit.*, p. 29.
24. *Ibid.*, pp. 28–9.
25. *Ibid.*, p. 30.
26. *Ibid.*, p. 31–2.
27. *Ibid*.
28. Hearne, K. M. T., *Visions of the Future*, Aquarian Press, UK, 1989, p. 64.
29. Inglis, B., *The Power of Dreams*, Paladin/Grafton Books, London, 1988, p. 1.
30. Hearne, K. M. T., *op. cit.*, p. 15.
31. *Ibid*.

Chapter 6

1. Becker, R. de, *The Understanding of Dreams*, George Allen & Unwin, London, 1968, p. 201.
2. Dee, N., *Your Dreams and What They Mean*, Aquarian Press, UK, 1984, p. 13.
3. *Ibid.*
4. *Ibid.*
5. Fornari, A., *How to Interpret Dreams*, Hamlyn Books, London, 1989, p. 13.
6. Inglis, B., *The Power of Dreams*, Paladin Grafton Books, London, 1987, p. 1.
7. Dee, N., *op. cit.*, p. 24.
8. Miller, G. H., *The Dictionary of Dreams*, Blaketon-Hall, Devon, 1983, p. 7.
9. Parker, R., *Healing Dreams*, SPCK, UK, 1988, p. 7.
10. *Ibid.*
11. Judges, 7, verses 13–14, New International Version (NIV)
12. Irwin, C. H., *The Universal Bible Commentary*, Religious Tract Society, 1894, p. 23.
13. Parker, R., *op. cit.*, p. 9.
14. Acts 10, v. 22 (RSV).
15. Becker, R. de, *op. cit.*, p. 29.
16. Saddhatissa, H., *The Life of the Buddha*, Allen & Unwin, London, 1976, p. 15.
17. Idowu, B. E., *African Traditional Religion*, SCM Press, London, 1973, p. 42.
18. Ullman, M. *et al.*, *Working with Dreams*, Aquarian Press, New York, 1987, p. 38.

Chapter 7

1. McWhirter, N., Guinness Book of Records, 1980, p. 4.
2. *The Hutchinson Encyclopedia*, 8th Edition, London, 1988.
3. *Encyclopaedia Britannica, Macropaedia*, University of Chicago, 1985, N. 14, p. 423.
4. Inglis, B., *The Power of Dreams*, Paladin Grafton Books, London, 1988, p. 29.
5. *Ibid.*, p. 29–30.
6. *Ibid.*, p. 51.
7. Lang, A., *The Book of Dreams and Ghosts*, London, 1897, p. 425.
8. Inglis, B., *Guardian*, September 1987.
9. Reed, H., *Getting Help from Your Dreams*, Inner Vision Publishing Co., Virginia Beach, 1988, p. 53.

10. Cayce, E., *The World's Greatest Psychic*, The Association of Research, UK, 1989, p. 38.
11. *Ibid.*, p. 39.
12. Inglis, B., *The Power of Dreams*, Paladin Grafton, London, 1988, p. 42.
13. Krippner, S., Ullman, M. and Vaughn, A., *Dream Telepathy*, Macmillan, New Yokr, 1973. Quoted in Cartwright, R. D. *Night Life*, Prentice-Hall, New Jersey, 1977, p. 3.
14. Cartwright, R. D., *Night Life*, Prentice-Hall, New Jersey, 1977, p. 3.
15. Mallon, B., *Women Dreaming*, William Collins Sons, UK, 1987, p. 223.
16. Becker, R. de., *The Understanding of Dreams*, George Allen & Unwin, London, 1968, p. 251.
17. *Ibid.*, p. 375.
18. *Ibid.*, p. 376.

Index

Abercrombie, John 120
Aborigines (Australia) 77, 119
Adebora, Lydia 62, 65–6
Adler, Alfred xv, 17–19, 84
Africa
  ATR (African Traditional
    Religion) 55–61, 77
  author's dream experiences in
    31–9
  cultural characteristics of 1–2
  societal beliefs xv, 53–73
African Traditional Religion (Idowu)
  68
Alexander the Great 94
Alonge, Charles 129–30
Alonge, Rachel 129
Amazulu of South Africa 67
ancestors, spirits of
  in Africa 54, 55, 56, 78
  among the Ngoni 25–6
  appearing in dreams 59–61
  worship of 62–3
animals, humans reborn as 78, 89
Apollo 91
archetypal imagery, in Jung 16–17,
  28, 37, 40, 115
Aristander 94
Aristotle 77, 92, 107
Artemidorus of Ephesus 90, 92,
  106
Asclepius 91
Aserinsky, Eugene 10, 11
Atkinson, Jose 96
ATR (African Traditional Religion)
  55–61, 77
Augustine, Saint 93–4, 107

Australia, aborigines 77, 119
author's dreams 30–53, 104–5
  in Africa 31–9
  of being anaemic 125
  in Britain 39–50
  of her brothers 45–6, 127, 130
  of her father 32, 34, 36–7, 124–5,
    130
  and her mother 32, 34, 35, 41–4,
    46
  of her sister 38–9, 88–9
  negative 34–6
  of other family members 36–9
  positive 32–4
  of self 32–6
Ayende (Gowa) 61

Babylon 106, 116
bad dreams, and the Ngoni 23
baptism, and born-again
  Christianity 76
Becker, Raymond de 6, 7, 116, 129
Bible, the, and reincarnation 75–6,
  89
Biblical dreams xv, 90, 106–15
Binder, Alma 49, 125
Bismarck, Count Otto von 94–5
Blackmore, Susan 2, 3, 11, 12
born-again Christianity 76
brothers of author, dreams of 45–6,
  127, 130
Bryden, Pat 16, 46, 48
Buddhism 77, 116, 117, 118
burials
  and death by burning 64
  and falling in trances 27–8

and ghosts 84
and life after death 57

Callaway, Rev. Canon 67, 69
Calpurnia 92
Carnston, Sylvia 87
Carpenter, Kimbundu Angola 73
Cartwright, R. D. 7, 9, 17, 28, 127
Cayce, Edgar 125–6
Cecilla Metella 107
Chapman, Mrs H. V. 98–9
Chewa 78
Chienda, Rev. 53
Chikhadzula, Margaret 49–50, 120
children, and death 85
children's dreams, among the
    Ngoni 21–3, 24, 36
Chingwanda, Margaret 89
Chingwanda, Phil 89
Chinkwita, Mary see author's
    dreams
Chinkwita, Oliver 63
Chinkwita, Stensfield 127
Christian ministry dreams 32–4,
    72–3
Christianity 118, born-again 76
Christianity
    early Christian views of dreams
    93
    and reincarnation 75–6, 77
Chuang-tzu 92–3
Chumbe, Dr Themba 104
Cicero 17
clairvoyants 129
Cole, George 70
collective unconscious, in Jung 16
Condoret, Marquis de 120
Cosgrove, Rita 45
Crick, Francis 1, 37, 106–7

dancing, and the Senoi 20, 21
day-dreaming 103–5
day-to-day problems 122–3
death, see also reincarnation
    author's dreams of 36–7, 38–9,
    41–4
    by burning 64

dreams believed to predict 49,
    71–2
    life after 57–61
decision-making
    dreams as aid in 124–5
    participation of the dead in 61
Dee, Nerys 11, 12, 90, 91
Delphi oracle 91
destiny, dreams as foretelling 19,
    21, 51, 53
devil, the 49
diviners 59, 65, 66
    and the Ngoni 23, 26, 28–9
Don's dreams, in the sleep
    laboratory 9
Dowd, Peter 2–3, 4
dramas, in dreams 19
dream time 119
Dreaming (Malcolm) 10
dreamlight machine 12
Dudley, G. A. 36, 41
Duggan, Mary 103–4
Durgan, Mary 16–17

Eeden, Frederick Van 2
ego, in Freud 12
Egypt, ancient, and dreams 90, 95,
    105, 106
Elijah 75, 89
essay writing 121
evil, dreams as warnings against
    26
examinations, dreams regarding
    14, 22, 120–1
externalist approach to dreams xiv,
    82, 84, 97

families, see also author's dreams
    death and rebirth within same
    58–61
Faraday, Ann 13, 31
father of author 32, 34
    death of 36–7
    as guardian spirit 124–5, 130
Ferguson, Jane 21, 37, 53, 102, 109
flying, dreams of 14, 72, 106
forefathers see ancestors
Forrest, Colin 120–1

fortune-tellers 74
Franz, Marie-Louise von 21, 51, 53, 109
Freud, Sigmund xiv, 1, 12–15, 28
  on telepathy 129
  The Interpretation of Dreams 94, 96, 105
  and wish-fulfilment 8, 13–14, 40, 98, 99, 102
funerals *see* burials
future, dreams as foretelling 15–16, 19, 28, 47, 49, 52, 55

Galen 91
Gande, Rev. 85
Garwell, Barbara 100
Gennadius 107
Georgeson, Pat 96
ghosts 84–5
Gideon 108, 118
God
  and ancestor worship 62, 63
  in ATR 54, 55–6
  and Christian ministry dreams 73
  dreams as messages from 26, 30–1, 37, 39, 105, 107–15
  and the early Christian views of dreams 93
Gondwe, Anne 68
Gordon, Thelma 100
graveyards 57, 58
Greeks, ancient
  and dreams 90, 91–2, 105
  and the soul 77, 78
Green, L. 4, 9
Gregory the Great 93
Gregory of Nyssar 93
guardian angels/spirits 119, 124–5
guide spirit (gunig) and the Senoi 20, 21
Gulf War 100–1

Hale Hall, dream of 80–2
healing, and trances 21
Hearne, Keith xiv, 2, 3, 4, 9, 14, 100, 104, 105
Hebrews 105

Hendrick, Emily 102
herbal medicines, and the Ngoni 26, 27, 28
herbalists/diviners 23, 26, 28–9
Herodotus 77
Heseltine, Michael 46, 47, 48
Hindeman, Gustavus Miller 49
Hinduism 77
Hippocrates xv, 92, 106
historical dreams 94–7
Historical Study of African Religion, The (Ranger and Kimambo) 26
Hitler, Adolf 94
hole in leg dream 41
Holfer, Hans 85
Holman, D. 18, 20
Homer 91
Howe, Elias 126–7
hunting dreams 66–7
hypnosis viii, 5–7, 10, 86, 92

Id, in Freud 12, 14
Idowu, B. E. 55, 68, 117
Igbinovia, Martha 47
illnesses
  curing of 65
  and dreams 55, 124–5
  imprisonment, dream of 48–9
individualisation, in Jung 15
Indonesia 77
Inglis, Brian 49, 90, 103, 107, 119, 122
instantaneous realisation 40
intermediaries
  in ATR 56–7
  in dreams 50–3
internalist approach to dreams 31, 84
  in Adler xv
interpretation of dreams, in Africa 65–6, 71–2
Interpretation of Dreams, The (Freud) 94, 96, 105
Irenaeus 93
Isaiah the Prophet 113–14
Islam 55, 56, 116, 117–18

Jacob (Old Testament) 108–10
Jal-wang, Grace xv, 30, 47, 50, 128, 130
Jaward, Mwajuma 52–3
Jerome, Saint 94
Jerry's dreams, in the sleep laboratory 7–9
Jesus Christ 56, 72, 85, 89, 112, 114, 117
  and reincarnation 75, 76
Johnson, Raynor 87
Johnston, Anne 126
Jones, Evelyn 46, 48
Joseph (New Testament) 112, 118
Joseph (Old Testament) 90, 110–12, 116, 118
Jouvet, M. 10
Judaeo-Christian culture 55, 56, 116, 118
Julius Caesar 92
Jung, Carl Gustav xiv, 1, 15–17, 21, 38, 39, 84, 129
  and the archetypal aspects of the dreamer 16–17, 28, 37, 40, 115
  Memories, Dreams, Reflections 78–9
  and reincarnation 78–9, 82, 83, 89
  on the unconscious mind 31

Kafumba, Angela 46, 68
Kafumba, Charles 46
Kala Devela 117
Kenya 55
Khan, Melanie 47
King, Martin Luther 115–16
Kleitman, Nathaniel 10, 11
Koran, the 117–18
Krippner, S. 127

LaBerge, Stephen 2, 12
laboratories, sleep xiii, 3–4, 5–12
Langley, Jackie 14
Lee, Barbara xv, 46, 48, 79–84, 89, 97–102
life after death 57–61
Ligomeka, Nelson 25
lost property, dreams of 121–2

lucid dreams 1–29
  natural 9, 29, 39, 47

Mabasa, Hannah (Mrs Kawalewale) 105, 124
McDermott, Maggie 4
McGuire, Sue 100–1
McManaman, Josephine 102
Magombo, Rev. 73
Magoun, H. W. 10
Major, John 47, 48
Malawi 1–2, 55
  dreaming the opposite in 103
  Ngoni of 2, 18, 21–9
  and reincarnation 78
Malaysia, Senoi (Temiar) people of xv, 1, 18–21, 23, 26, 29
Malcolm, N. 10
male dreams, among the Senoi 19
Mallon, Brenda 127–8
malombo (spirit possession) 21, 25–6
marriage in dreams
  among the Ngoni 24
  among the Senoi 19
  of author's brother 45–6
  of Grace Jal-wang 50–1
  weddings 24, 45–6, 72
Marriott, Gladys 4
Mary (mother of Jesus) 112, 118
mashawi (vibanda) 25
Maury, Alfred 11
Maya (mother of Buddha) 117
Mbiti, John 54, 62
Mbonya, Margaret 66
Medawar, Peter 1, 37
medicine dreams 67–8
Melanesia 77
Memories, Dreams, Reflections (Jung) 78–9
Mesopotamian literature 106
messages
  dreams as bearing 17, 26, 30–1, 37, 39
  and African beliefs 54, 55
Micronesia 77
Middle Ages 93–4, 105

atissa, H. 117
e, Sandra 47, 71
, Nellie 124
ya, Charles 58–9, 60
Sir Walter 122
(Temiar) people of Malaysia
, 1, 18–21, 23, 26, 29
aim 113–14
experience in dreams 19
speare, William 95
s, in ancient Greece 91
Leone 55
s, Elizabeth 86
on, George 66
ng on it (problems) 122, 123
ng laboratories xiii, 3–4,
-12, 30
, Moreen 42
s, dreaming of 49
es 77, 91–2, 105

the Ngoni 26
reincarnation 77–9
the Senoi 20
possession, see also
ncestors, spirits of; guardian
ngels/spirits
ong the Ngoni 25–6
ong the Senoi 20–1
David 62, 66
nscious see unconscious
iind
n 55
kler, Bengt 72
ego 12
iority complexes, in Jung
7–18
rland, S. 1, 28
ols, in dreams 19
onicity 128

r, J. V. 67
t, Norman 46, 48
thy 119, 127–30
ir see Senoi people of
Malaysia

Tempest, The (Shakespeare) 95
Tertullian 94
Thadzi, Joyce 124
Thatcher, Margaret 46–8
trances, among the Senoi 21, 27–9
trees, dreams of 72
twins, dreams of 60–1

Ullman, Montague 51, 115, 118,
127
ultra-paradoxical phase, in sleep
laboratories 6
unconscious mind xiv
in Freud 40
and the future 36
in Jung 15–17, 31
universality of dreams 53

Vaughn, A. 127
verification of dreams 31
vibanda (mashawi) 25
Victoria, Queen 119
vimbuza 25
visions, in the Bible 112–15
Visions of the Future (Hearne) 104

war dreams 100–1
warnings, Biblical dreams as
110–12
Waterman, Monica 46
weddings, see also marriage in
dreams
dreams of 24, 45–6, 72
Welsh, and reincarnation 77
Whisson, M. G. 59
wish-fulfilment dreams, in Freud
xiv, 8, 13–14, 40, 98, 99, 102
witchcraft dreams 68–9
witches 85
Women Dreaming (Mallon) 127–8
Worsley, Alan 3–4

Yates, Lorraine 42

zero RR (realisation rate) 107
Zimba, George 86–7

Miller, Gustavus Hindman 45, 92, 107
morality, teaching of, and dreams 23
Moruzzi, Giuseppe 10
Mothea, Nchafatso 64–5
mother of author 32, 34, 35, 36
    dreams of death of 41–4
Mtalika, Sultan 58
Muhammad (prophet) 56, 117–18
Mulenga, Rev. 33
Munthali, Matilda, 57
Murray, David Christie 84, 86
mystical power, in African villages 28

nakedness dream 39–41
Nambewe, Mai 58
Napoleon Bonaparte 94
Natsothe, Mai 70
natural lucid dreams 9, 29, 39, 47
Ndongela, Mai 24
Near-Death Experience 74
New Testament 105, 112, 118
Ngoni of Malawi 2, 18, 21–9
Nigeria 55
Night Life (Cartwright) 7, 28, 127
nightmares 126
Ninevah 106
NREM (non-REM) sleep state 12
nsembe (thanksgiving) 26

Old Testament 90, 93, 105, 108–12, 113–14, 116, 118
Omen, the 24–5
opposite, dreaming the 102–3
oracles 56
organ inferiority 18
Origen 93

Pacific Islands 77
parables, in dreams 19
Parker, R. 112
Parrinder, E. G. P. 55
Paul the Apostle 76, 114, 115
Peak, A. S. 76
Peter (Apostle) 113
Peters, Professor 128

Pikiti, Joackin
Plato xv, 12,
Plutarch 92
Polycarp 93
Popper, Karl
premonitions,
    97–102
priests 56–7
    and the inte
    65–6
Primitive Relig
problem-solve
    xv–xvi, 11
prophecy 107,
    possessio
prophets 56
    in the Bible
Purvis, Phil 75

Ragbourn, Bri
Ranger and Ki
Rapid Eye Mo
    3–4, 6, 10,
realisation rate
Reed, Henry 1
reincarnation ×
religion, see als
    in Africa 54,
    dreams as m
    115–16
    dreams of 32
Religious and S
    Southern A
Reticular Activ
    10
Richet, Charles
riddles, in drea
Romans
    and dreams
    107
    Paul's letter
Rowie, R. H. 6
Ruddock, Stan

sacrifices, and
    62–3
Sadat, Anwar,
    100

Sadd
St Ro
Saka
Saka
Scott
Seno

serap
sexu
Shak
shrin
Sierr
Simr
Simp
sleep
sleep

Smit
snak
Socr
souls
    an
    an
    an
spiri

an
an
Sten
subc

Suda
Sun
supe
supe

Suth
sym
sync

Tay
Teb
tele
Ten